HIDDEN IN MY HEART
A Study of Psalms 119

Marvin McKenzie

All rights reserved.
@2022

For written permission to use this material, please contact Dr. Marvin McKenzie at marvin@marvinmckenzie.org

Years ago, when I first started in the ministry, I was admonished not to teach through Psalms 119. The reason, I think was with good intent. I was going to start a brand-new church and the pastor who encouraged me not to teach this wanted me to teach through Acts – it's an exciting book about church planting.

I just want to tell you that there may not be any more important portion of the Bible than Psalms 119. It sits right in the center of your Bible. It's the largest chapter in the Bible by far. Almost twice as long as the next longest.

May our loving Saviour bless a good meditation of this, most exciting piece of HIS WORD.

Chapter One
LET ME COUNT THE WAYS
Psalms 119:9 (KJV)
Wherewithal shall a young man cleanse his way? by taking heed thereto according to thy word.

QUESTIONS ABOUT THE WRITER
Psalms 118 is the center chapter of the Bible, but this is awfully close.

There is nothing in the passage to give a definite answer to this.

While most of the Psalms were written by David, there are several of them that were composed by others.

- **Ethan the Ezrahite**
- **Heman the Ezrahite**
- **Asaph**
- **The sons of Korah and even**
- **Moses and**
- **Solomon**

contributed to them.

Some Bible commentaries even suggest that Psalms 119 may not have a single author but might be a collection of phrases and wise sayings that were compiled together to form the work.

I think that is unlikely because of the poetic nature and strong "structure" of the Psalm.

It doesn't matter or else God would have told us specifically who He used to give us this piece of inspiration.

I think it is likely David. It bears small passages that sound to me like other things we know that David wrote.

QUESTIONS ABOUT WHEN IT WAS WRITTEN

By the way, just so you don't think this is a waste of time to consider, remember that one of the first things a Bible student must do if he is to properly interpret the Bible is to ask the questions

- **Who was the writer?**
- **To whom was he writing?**
- **What were the circumstances at the time of the writing?**

While we are not always given the precise answers to these questions for every passage – it is an important consideration.

- **All Scripture is given by the inspiration of God.**
- **God saw to it that it is preserved in the Word of God**

It is important to know whether it is God Himself speaking, or the devil.

Those who believe the Psalm to be a collection of wise sayings – sort of like proverbs only focused on just one topic – think it may have been written over hundreds of years, even after the Babylonian captivity.

I see it more like David's "opus."

David was a prolific writer all of his life. Some of the things he wrote were very short and to the point. I can see him sitting down with quill and parchment and penning Psalm 23 in a few moments.

I had poems come to my mind in the middle of the night while driving so that I pull over at a rest stop so I can write the words down. Mark Lowry came up with the words to the well-known Christmas song, "Mary Did You Know?" while sleeping on a music group's bus, traveling from one gig to the next. He said he woke up one of the other guys, sang it off the top of his head and the rest, as they say, is history.

On the other hand, there are some things that take much more time and thought. I see David perhaps beginning this as a young man and working on it for the better part of his life.

QUESTIONS ABOUT THE STRUCTURE
Okay, well, there really aren't any questions about the structure. I just gave it that heading for the continuity of my outline.

It is an amazing piece of the Bible because there is such a strong structure to it
A. There are twenty-two stanzas, each one beginning (in the Hebrew) with the next letter I the sequence of the Hebrew alphabet.

B. Each stanza contains eight lines.
In most cases the verses of our Bible are not inspired but simply divided into chapters and verses for our study help. That is not the case with the Psalms because they are individual psalms. And it is not the case with the verses of this Psalm because they are individual lines. Each one of the eight lines in each stanza begin with the same Hebrew letter.

C. There are a total of one hundred seventy-six verses.

D. There is only one verse that does not clearly reference the Bible.

E. None of them are the same.
There are one hundred seventy-five declarations about the Bible and not one of them is a repeat.

It's like it's an exercise
F. How many ways can we praise God for His Word?

Psalms 119:122 (KJV)
Be surety for thy servant for good: let not the proud oppress me.

The different words used to refer to the Bible include Law, Word. Judgments, testimonies, commandments, statutes, and precepts.

You cannot put too much attention on the Bible.
It should be the meditation of your lifetime.

Chapter Two
IT'S ALL BIBLE

Psalms 119:1-9 (KJV)

Blessed are the undefiled in the way, who walk in the law of the LORD.

Blessed are they that keep his testimonies, and that seek him with the whole heart.

They also do no iniquity: they walk in his ways.

Thou hast commanded us to keep thy precepts diligently.

O that my ways were directed to keep thy statutes!

Then shall I not be ashamed, when I have respect unto all thy commandments.

I will praise thee with uprightness of heart, when I shall have learned thy righteous judgments.

I will keep thy statutes: O forsake me not utterly.

Wherewithal shall a young man cleanse his way? by taking heed thereto according to thy word.

There are nine words in all. Eight of them are found in the first nine verses of Psalms 119. I am going to take them in alphabetical order. The nineth one is found in Psalms 119:91. It has a uniqueness to it that caused me to set it apart.

COMMANDMENTS

Psalms 119:6 (KJV)

Then shall I not be ashamed, when I have respect unto all thy commandments.

You've probably noticed that every one of these has the same three points to work with. I used the Webster's 1828 dictionary and supplemented with an online version of a modern Webster's in a few cases where I needed some help.

Webster's

A command; a mandate; an order or injunction **given by authority**; charge; precept.

Strong's
To command, charge, **give orders**, lay charge, give charge to, order

Ancient Hebrew
To commit to one's **charge**[1]

We might think of the commandments as the Ten Commandments. After doing this study I would suggest that it is not a reference to the Ten Commandments unless the context specifically points to them.

JUDGMENTS
Psalms 119:7 (KJV)
I will praise thee with uprightness of heart, when I shall have learned thy righteous judgments.

Webster's
Determination; decision.

Strong's
a *verdict* (favorable or unfavorable) pronounced judicially, especially a *sentence* or formal decree.

Ancient Hebrew
To make a **verbal** decision.[2]

Note the concept of verbal. Sometimes we "judge" someone or something, but it results in how we respond. This is a judgment it isn't an attitude we have based on a secretly judging. It is an action we expect based on a communicated decision.

---

[1] This came from Webster's etymology and not the Ancient Hebrew.
[2] Also from Webster's etymology

LAW
Psalms 119:1 (KJV)
Blessed are the undefiled in the way, who walk in the law of the LORD.

Webster's
A rule, particularly **an established or permanent rule**, prescribed by the supreme power of a state to its subjects.

Strong's
The word is Torah, a *precept* or *statute*, especially the *Decalogue* or *Pentateuch:*

This is the whole of the first five books of the Bible. It is not the Ten Commandments. It is all of the commandments as well as those things taught in the rest of those first five books.

They are established and permanent. God has preserved them. They are accurate, without error and profitable for our study.

Ancient Hebrew
The pictograph is a man's hand. The idea is that of pointing direction.

The first five books of the Bible, we call it the *Pentateuch,* sets the course for everything else we learn in the Word of God.

PRECEPTS
Psalms 119:4 (KJV)
Thou hast commanded us to keep thy precepts diligently.

Webster's

Any commandment or order intended as an authoritative rule of action; but applied particularly to commands respecting **moral conduct**.

Strong's
Appointed, that is, a *mandate* (of God)

Ancient Hebrew
To oversee, give direction for a purpose or product.

Because of these definitions, I think we could think of them as specifically the Ten Commandments.

STATUTES
Psalms 119:5 (KJV)
O that my ways were directed to keep thy statutes!

Psalms 119:8 (KJV)
I will keep thy statutes: O forsake me not utterly.

Webster's
An act of the legislature of a state that extends its binding force **to all the citizens** or subjects of that state, as distinguished from an act which extends only to an individual or company.

Strong's
Something **prescribed**, due[3]

Ancient Hebrew
A rule designed to bring together, a custom that all are expected to uphold.

---

[3] From Brown-Driver-Briggs

I can't help but think about the local church here. "A called out assembly of baptized believers united together for a common purpose"

TESTIMONIES
Psalms 119:2 (KJV)
Blessed are they that keep his testimonies, and that seek him with the whole heart.

Webster's
A solemn declaration or affirmation made for the purpose of establishing or proving some fact.

Strong's
Concretely, *a witness*; abstractly *testimony*; specifically a *recorder*

It is something written and given under oath, certified by a witness.[4]

Ancient Hebrew
A place, time or event that is **repeated** again and again.

As in people gather together to hear it repeated.
I think of the preaching of the Word of God

WAYS
Psalms 119:3 (KJV)
They also do no iniquity: they walk in his ways.

Webster's
A **road** of any kind

Strong's
A *course* **of life** or *mode of* action,

---

[4] Like a notary public

Ancient Hebrew
A **journey** as a treading. The stringing of a bow is a treading as the foot is stepped over the bow and using the leg to bend it.

I'm thinking of instructions on where to place my feet so that I end up where God wants me.

WORD
Psalms 119:9 (KJV)
Wherewithal shall a young man cleanse his way? by taking heed thereto according to thy word.

Webster's
The message delivered by **word of mouth**.

Strongs
a *cause:* - act, advice

Consider that advice isn't meant to be just another opinion you hear, it is meant to cause you to act upon it.

Ancient Hebrew
An arrangement or placement of something **creating order**.

The Word of God was written over the course of over 1400 years by more than 40 different men.
It is a collection of 66 books.
But they have such order and unity as to testify to only 1 author, God.

When we submit to its teachings, it gives order to our lives.

ORDINANCES

Psalms 119:91 (KJV)
They continue this day according to thine ordinances: for all are thy servants.

Webster's
Established rite or **ceremony**.

Strong's
A particular *right*, or *privilege* (statutory or customary), or even a *style:* - ceremony

Ancient Hebrew
Manner, right, cause, ordinance, lawful, order, worthy, fashion, **custom**

This is the same Hebrew word that is translated judgments above except, I think, the focus is on ceremonial aspect of its definition.

We speak of the two ordinances of the New Testament Baptist Church:
- **Baptism and**
- **Lord's Supper**

They do not contribute to our salvation, but God has delivered a determination that we should obey them.

Chapter Three
THEY WALK IN HIS WAYS
Psalms 119:1-8 (KJV) ALEPH.
Blessed are the undefiled in the way, who walk in the law of the LORD. Blessed are they that keep his testimonies, and that seek him with the whole heart.
They also do no iniquity: they walk in his ways.
Thou hast commanded us to keep thy precepts diligently.
O that my ways were directed to keep thy statutes!
Then shall I not be ashamed, when I have respect unto all thy commandments.
I will praise thee with uprightness of heart, when I shall have learned thy righteous judgments.
I will keep thy statutes: O forsake me not utterly.

There is no intrinsic evidence that David wrote Psalms 119, it does have some elements that sound like other things David did write. That leads me to believe he is the writer. This Psalm begins like something else David wrote begins. Imagine, for just moment that Psalms 119 is its own book of the Bible.[5] Imagine, for instance, that the Bible contained:

- **1 and 2 Samuel**
- **1 and 2 Kings**
- **1 and 2 Chronicles and**
- **1 and 2 Psalms[6]**

With that in mind, let's compare Psalms 119:1-2[7] and Psalms 1:1-2[8] I am going to call this stanza, **They That Walk In His Ways**

---

[5] It should not be difficult to imagine since it is as big or bigger than other books of the Bible.

[6] I know that it doesn't.

[7] Psalms 119:1-2 (KJV)

Blessed are the undefiled in the way, who walk in the law of the LORD.

They that walk in His ways
ARE BLESSED
Psalms 119:1-4 (KJV)
Blessed are the undefiled in the way, who walk in the law of the LORD. Blessed are they that keep his testimonies, and that seek him with the whole heart.
They also do no iniquity: they walk in his ways.
Thou hast commanded us to keep thy precepts diligently.

Most of the time we think of the word "blessed" as one who has unusual favor.
-Someone whose life just seems to always work out:
- **Blessed to have good parents**
- **Blessed to have a good education** • **Blessed to be in good health**

We, who are Christians, will often use the word "blessed" to mean, **the generosity and favor of God**.

Really the word just means, "**happy**." If you think about the two definitions, it absolutely changes the meaning of these verses.

One of them is an attempt to get God to do something for us.
- **If I am undefiled**
- **If I walk in the Law of the Lord**
- **If I keep His testimonies**
- **If I seek Him with my whole heart** • **If I don't sin and**

Blessed are they that keep his testimonies, and that seek him with the whole heart.
[8] Psalms 1:1-2 (KJV)
Blessed is the man that walketh not in the counsel of the ungodly, nor standeth in the way of sinners, nor sitteth in the seat of the scornful.
But his delight is in the law of the LORD; and in his law doth he meditate day and night.

- **If I diligently keep His precepts**

Then God will do good things for me.
Look at it this way:
- **If I am undefiled**
- **If I walk in the Law of the Lord**
- **If I keep His testimonies**
- **If I seek Him with my whole heart • If I don't sin and**
- **If I diligently keep His precepts**

Then I will be a happy person.

The first use is selfish **and manipulative** – and it could backfire if God doesn't pour out all the good things you hope for.

The other one offers just **good instructions**.
A person who walks with the Lord is going to be happier in this life than the person who is defiled and lives a life of iniquity.

By the way, a person who walks with the Lord because He is the Lord, will be much happier in life than the person who walks with the Lord because he wants something from God.

They that walk in His ways
ARE DIRECTED
Psalms 119:5-6 (KJV)
O that my ways were directed to keep thy statutes!
Then shall I not be ashamed, when I have respect unto all thy commandments.

I think this goes to my original point that the blessed man is one who follows God's instructions. The idea of direction is to have things in **order and arranged**. I notice that this passage is a **plea** and not a **declaration**. He is begging God to help him or direct him to keep God's statutes. That's purely wisdom and humility.

One of the things that is true of us and that we are most likely to deny is that **our nature is at war with God.** It's like this – **as much as we know** that the happiest, we will be is when we walk in the ways of the Lord, **that is the last thing** that we will do if we have our way.

Have you ever met a stubborn and proud Christian?
"I know what God wants, and that is exactly what I am going to do!"

The Psalmist had exactly the opposite spirit.
He knew the most blessed people are those who walk in the way so, he prayed for God to direct him to walk that way .

A spiritually proud person might come under conviction during a message and come forward at the altar and pray something like this,
"Lord thank you for teaching me your Word today. From now on I promise to
do what You taught me."

I believe the Psalmist would have come to the same altar after the same message and prayed more like this,
"Lord thank you for teaching me your
Word today. O Lord order my steps and arrange my life so that I am able to do what You taught me."

They that walk in His ways
ARE NOT FORSAKEN
Psalms 119:7-8 (KJV)
I will praise thee with uprightness of heart, when I shall have learned thy righteous judgments.
I will keep thy statutes: O forsake me not utterly.

If I transition from verse five, **"Lord direct my steps"** then verse six **will be true of me, "I am not ashamed"** because through the power of the Lord, verse seven **"I am able to learn His righteous judgments and to praise God."** And that leads me to this realization, verse eight **"God does not forsake us utterly."**

I know that for a fact because the Bible says, Deuteronomy 4:31 (KJV)
(For the LORD thy God is a merciful God;) he will not forsake thee, neither destroy thee, nor forget the covenant of thy fathers which he sware unto them. And in the New Testament[9] Hebrews 13:5 (KJV)
Let your conversation be without covetousness; and be content with such things as ye have: for he hath said, I will never leave thee, nor forsake thee.

Which person is most likely to be happy?
- **The person who lives trying to do good things so God will give Him good things and won't forsake him? Or**
- **The person who because He walks in the ways of the Lord knows that**

God has promised him that He will bless him and won't ever forsake him?
I want to be the latter of these, don't you?

That leads us back to verse five where we learn to pray for God to direct our ways, our thoughts, our hearts so that:
- **His Word is first in our life and**
- **By faith we accept that He is**
- **blessing us and**
- **We trust He will never forsake us**

---

[9] There are at least six times the Bible says that God will not forsake us.

Chapter Four

TAKING HEED

Psalms 119:9-16 (KJV) BETH.

Wherewithal shall a young man cleanse his way? by taking heed thereto according to thy word.
With my whole heart have I sought thee: O let me not wander from thy commandments.
Thy word have I hid in mine heart, that I might not sin against thee.
Blessed art thou, O LORD: teach me thy statutes.
With my lips have I declared all the judgments of thy mouth.
I have rejoiced in the way of thy testimonies, as much as in all riches.
I will meditate in thy precepts, and have respect unto thy ways.
I will delight myself in thy statutes: I will not forget thy word.

I'm thinking about those "golden nuggets" of Scripture we find scattered throughout the Word of God. The Bible is a book worthy of study and deep meditation. There are truths buried so deep in the Word of God that, should we spend an entire lifetime researching them out, we will not exhaust the resources.

The Bible is such a rich book that we will spend all of eternity sitting at the throne of God while He teaches us things in this Book we cannot dream of today. But then, just for our pleasure and because we are such a needy people, the Lord has seen fit to give us in every book of the Bible and on almost every page of the Bible certain treasures of various sizes and shapes, clear to the eye and easy for the picking.

This passage contains two of them[10] – one of which I believe to be the key to this stanza of the Psalm.

Psalms 119:9(KJV)

Wherewithal shall a young man cleanse his way? by taking heed thereto according to thy word.

---

[10] Psalms 119:11 (KJV)
Thy word have I hid in mine heart, that I might not sin against thee.

- There is a query[11] and
- There is a solution[12]

Albert Barnes says of this verse, "*There can be no more important inquiry for one just entering on the journey of life; there can be found nowhere a more just and comprehensive answer than is contained in this single verse.*"

The solution is expanded upon in the remaining verses of the stanza.

How is it that we take heed according to God's Word?

WITH THE WHOLE HEART

Psalms 119:10 (KJV)

With my whole heart have I sought thee: O let me not wander from thy commandments.

I wonder how many of us could claim that we have sought the Lord with our whole heart? I imagine there would be more of us who would confess that we would like to do that but have not attained it as well as we would wish.

Notice with me some key concepts scattered through these eight verses:

A. Hide the Word in my heart

Psalms 119:11 (KJV)

Thy word have I hid in mine heart, that I might not sin against thee.

I know of no other way to apply that except to memorize the Word of God. Notice where you hide it, not in your brain but in your heart.

- **The Bible is not a book of facts that you file away.**

---

[11] Psalms 119:9a (KJV)

Wherewithal shall a young man cleanse his way

[12] Psalms 119:9b (KJV)

... by taking heed thereto according to thy word.

- **The Bible is a letter of love that you cherish always.**[13]

I have engaged in Bible memory programs.
- **I don't mind them and have even given them out. The Treasure Path to Soulwinning is a good one to use.**
- **At one time I memorized a chapter of the Bible a week and quoted it to Bro George Simmons every Sunday night.**[14]

But the passages that I have memorized the most readily, and the ones that I can recall most easily, are those that were not a part of a plan for memory but because I got so blessed by the passage that I grew to love it.

B. Rejoice in God's Word
Psalms 119:14 (KJV)
I have rejoiced in the way of thy testimonies, as much as in all riches.

The word means to **exult in** or to be *cheered by*.
That's a heart thing.

It is not difficult to spend time with something that brings you joy and cheer.
C. Delight in God's Word
Psalms 119:16 (KJV)
I will delight myself in thy statutes: I will not forget thy word.

The word "delight" means "to watch over and to care for, as a shepherd would his flock of sheep."

---

[13] This is why the unsaved don't get the Bible. It is also why the saved can't convince the unsaved of its truthfulness by listing facts about the Bible.

[14] I asked Brother George to let me quote them to him because he was intimidating, and I knew I would be less likely to make excuses if he was the one, I was accountable to.

Imagine the shepherd on the hillside. His flock is before him. He sees them, but he also sees the landscape they are on, the fields and whether the pasture is fit, and other wildlife and if any of them pose a danger to his flock. He sees his flock in context to their surroundings. That's how I think we ought to see the word of God.

We see verse nine in the context of the rest of the stanza.

How is it that we take heed according to God's Word?
WITH FERVENT PRAYER
In this case, there are two verses to consider:
A. O let me not wander Psalms 119:10 (KJV)
With my whole heart have I sought thee: O let me not wander from thy commandments.

As much as we might love the Word of God, we are well aware of how prone to wander from it that we are.

We need the Lord's help to have a fervent heart of love for the Word of God.
B. Teach me thy statutes
Psalms 119:12 (KJV)
Blessed art thou, O LORD: teach me thy statutes.

I am glad to report that the Bible promises God will teach us His Word.
- **He teaches us the Word of God through our careful study**
- **He teaches us the Word of God through our pastors and teachers and**
- **He teaches us the Word of God through the guidance of the Holy Spirit who lives within us.**

How is it that we take heed according to God's Word?
WITH FAITHFULNESS
We take heed to the Word of God by being faithful and consistent in it.

There are three verses relevant to this point.
I want to change the order they are located to try to point out a progression.

A. Meditate in God's Word
Psalms 119:15 (KJV)
I will meditate in thy precepts, and have respect unto thy ways.

To meditate means to think over and over. It's more than memorizing – better really than memorizing. It's to keep a portion of the Word of God in front of you for a period of time so you can know it intimately.

B. Declare God's Word
Psalms 119:13 (KJV)
With my lips have I declared all the judgments of thy mouth.

Once I know something of the Word of God, the next step is to tell it to others. Pastor Scudder advised me, when he gave me a Sunday school class to teach, to study a passage of Scripture over and over until I could tell it in my own words.

That's all I've ever wanted our teachers to do.

C. Forget not God's Word
Psalms 119:16 (KJV)
I will delight myself in thy statutes: I will not forget thy word.

When you have learned a passage of Scripture well enough to teach it to others, you will be much less likely to forget it.

And more importantly, less likely to forget to take heed to it.

Chapter Five

THAT I MAY LIVE and Keep Thy Word

Psalms 119:17-24 (KJV) GIMEL.

Deal bountifully with thy servant, that I may live, and keep thy word.
Open thou mine eyes, that I may behold wondrous things out of thy law.
I am a stranger in the earth: hide not thy commandments from me.
My soul breaketh for the longing that it hath unto thy judgments at all times. Thou hast rebuked the proud that are cursed, which do err from thy commandments.
Remove from me reproach and contempt; for I have kept thy testimonies.
Princes also did sit and speak against me: but thy servant did meditate in thy statutes.
Thy testimonies also are my delight and my counsellors.

There are a couple of different ways to understand verse seventeen.

I imagine the most common way to view it would to that the Psalmist asks God to give him bountiful things to make life enjoyable, and that would make it easier for him to keep God's word. I do not believe that is the heartbeat of the Psalmist or of the Lord who inspired him.

Consider one hundred seventy-five verses in this Psalm describing the blessedness and the treasure that the Bible is. It would be much more consistent to understand that the Psalmist is asking the Lord to deal bountifully, to bless him in such a way that he would be able to live in a way that he keeps God's word.

It occurs to me that many of the conflicts, we have are over this very difference. In any given church there are

- **People trying to make the Bible fit with their life and**
- **People trying to make their life fit with the Bible**

They both believe the same doctrines amen the same sermons teach classes in the same Sunday school. But one of them believes the other one is a legalist and "too heavenly minded for any earthly good."

A pastor friend of mine was sitting in his office recently, preparing to preach the evening message. The deacons of his church came into his office unannounced, gave him a letter of resignation, and told him if he did not read it, they would publicly fire him without further compensation from the church. He was told if he wanted to leave town with a dime to his name, he could say nothing from the pulpit except what the letter said and that he was not allowed to speak to any member of the church, or they would refuse him a severance check. Once he read the letter the deacons came to the pulpit and announced that any member of the church who attempted to speak to the pastor would face disciplinary action from them.

My relationship with the church is such that I spent the bulk of Monday trying to help the members of the church – who were blindsided by these deacons. By Monday night all of the deacons but one had realized what they did was wrong and had resigned. By Tuesday morning another preacher connected with the church had flown in from out of state so there were boots on the ground. Wednesday night the deacons (except the one) publicly repented and the pastor's forced resignation was tossed out. The one who refused to repent said, "We may have gone about it the wrong way, but our intentions were good."

Here's the thing- none of them even considered what the Bible said was the role of the pastor, the role of the deacon or the role of the church.

- **They assumed that they had been elected as deacons to protect the church from the pastor**
- **They assumed they had authority to offer a severance check if he complied to them and**
- **They assumed they had the authority to refuse him his next paycheck if he did not**

You see, they assumed good intentions outweighed biblical instructions.

This is an incredibly egregious illustration of what the Psalmist presents in verse seventeen. We are so prone to put what we believe to be "good" above what the Bible teaches to be "right."

We desperately need God to deal bountifully with us so that avoid the corrupt nature, of seeing for ourselves what is good and evil,[15] and surrendering ourselves to what the Bible actually teaches.

The Psalmist asked that God deal bountifully with him. What would that look like?

OPENED EYES

Psalms 119:18 (KJV)
Open thou mine eyes, that I may behold wondrous things out of thy law.

- **We are so blind to the things of God.**
- **We are so conformed to the wisdom of this world.**

Except that God deals bountifully with us and opens our eyes, some of the most wonderful things in God's Word can't get past what we already think is right and good.

---

[15] Genesis 3:5 (KJV)
For God doth know that in the day ye eat thereof, then your eyes shall be opened, and ye shall be as gods, knowing good and evil.

The word law here might be relevant. Unless God opens our eyes His Word just looks like rules.

REVEALED COMMANDMENTS
Psalms 119:19 (KJV)
I am a stranger in the earth: hide not thy commandments from me.

When God deals bountifully with us, we see things in the Bible we have not seen before.

For years my wife has had this little tradition of hiding plastic eggs with candy (or money) in our yard for the kids to find. We do not do it the weekend of Resurrection Sunday, but we wanted our kids and now our grandkids, to enjoy the game. Every year there are eggs we hide so well that we find them all year long.

We're not going to find all the treasures God has in the Word of God in this lifetime. But we can pray every day that He reveals new ones to us.

NEARNESS TO THE WORD
Psalms 119:20 (KJV)
My soul breaketh for the longing that it hath unto thy judgments at all times.

I am reminded of Psalms 42:1 (KJV)
As the hart panteth after the water brooks, so panteth my soul after thee, O God.

This kind of love for God and His Word does not come naturally. If we have a measure of it, it is because God has dealt bountifully with us.

HUMILITY OVER PRIDE
Psalms 119:21 (KJV)

Thou hast rebuked the proud that are cursed, which do err from thy commandments.

It is a gracious and bountiful thing when God rebukes our pride and gives us the humility to put His Word of our wisdom.

REMOVED REPROACH
Psalms 119:22-23 (KJV)
Remove from me reproach and contempt; for I have kept thy testimonies.
Princes also did sit and speak against me: but thy servant did meditate in thy statutes.

King David faced the contempt of certain people all the days of his life. More important than that we have no one who reproaches us, is that our heart does not.
1 John 3:21 (KJV)
Beloved, if our heart condemn us not, then have we confidence toward God.

THE BIBLE IS OUR COUNSEL
Psalms 119:24 (KJV)
Thy testimonies also are my delight and my counsellors.

Rather than it being a book of general guidelines we use to walk the path we set, when God deals bountifully with us, we find our path in it.

Chapter Six

FAITH 101

Psalms 119:25-32 (KJV) DALETH

My soul cleaveth unto the dust: quicken thou me according to thy word.

I have declared my ways, and thou heardest me: teach me thy statutes.

Make me to understand the way of thy precepts: so shall I talk of thy wondrous works.

My soul melteth for heaviness: strengthen thou me according unto thy word.

Remove from me the way of lying: and grant me thy law graciously.

I have chosen the way of truth: thy judgments have I laid before me.

I have stuck unto thy testimonies: O LORD, put me not to shame.

I will run the way of thy commandments, when thou shalt enlarge my heart.

I want to call the fourth stanza of Psalms 119, "**Faith 101**." This is just generally good counsel of any Christian who longs to be more than a token Christian. There are at least four keys I find in these verses.

A BROKEN SOUL

Psalms 119:25 (KJV)

My soul cleaveth unto the dust: quicken thou me according to thy word.

Psalms 119:28 (KJV)

My soul melteth for heaviness: strengthen thou me according unto thy word.

In each of these I see:

A. An Object

The Hebrew word for soul means, "the whole being."
Our mind, our will, and our emotions.

Somewhere I learned to view the three parts of a man as

- **The Spirit** – that part of us that looks heavenward (communicates with God)
- **The soul** – that part of us that looks horizontally (communicates with those around us)
- **The body** – that part of us that looks earthward (communicates with nature or the natural)

Probably the most basic understanding of the soul is that it is our life.

In the case of mankind, life is a gift given by God.

Genesis 2:7 (KJV)

And the LORD God formed man of the dust of the ground, and breathed into his nostrils the breath of life; and man became a living soul.

b. An Action

Two actions of the soul are noted in this stanza
- **My soul cleaveth**
- **My soul melteth**

When I think of the word cleave, I think of a cleaver, something that separate or tears apart.[16] The word means, and in the context, it is obvious, to stick to, adhere to, to join together.

To melt means to leak, to weep or to pour out.

C. An Adverb

Two of them are here
- *"unto the dust"*
- *"for heaviness"*

I do not believe a Christian has to always be unhappy. But he ought to always remember he comes from the dust of the

---

[16] A modern thesaurus offered: chop, cut, slice, slash, and sever as possible alternatives.

ground, and every day a little bit more of him has been given back to the ground.

Psalms 90:12 (KJV)
So teach us to number our days, that we may apply our hearts unto wisdom.

Given our temporary status on this planet, the priority of every minute ought to be to know the LORD as we find Him in His WORD.

A WILLING TALK
Psalms 119:26 (KJV)
I have declared my ways, and thou heardest me: teach me thy statutes.

Psalms 119:27 (KJV)
Make me to understand the way of thy precepts: so shall I talk of thy wondrous works.

Psalms 119:29 (KJV)
Remove from me the way of lying: and grant me thy law graciously.

The progression I see in these three verses sounds a little bit like this:
A. Seek the Lord about the concerns of life
One of my commentaries says, "I have made mention of my cares, troubles, anxieties, purposes. I have laid them all before thee..." the good part is the assurance "thou heardest me."

B. Say nothing that is not true
The only thing I know is true is the Bible. I need to season everything I say with the Word of God.

C. Speak often about what God has done and is doing

Way too often our Christianity is about what we are doing or what someone else has done. Our heart needs to be filled with God, so our conversations are more about him.

A DETERMINED WALK
Psalms 119:30-32 (KJV)
I have chosen the way of truth: thy judgments have I laid before me
I have stuck unto thy testimonies: O LORD, put me not to shame.
I will run the way of thy commandments, when thou shalt enlarge my heart.

I see three wise choices here:
A. I have chosen the way of truth
Every human being has that choice
Proverbs 16:25 (KJV)
There is a way that seemeth right unto a man, but the end thereof are the ways of death.

Or the way of truth.

Joshua admonished the people of his time. Joshua 24:15 (KJV)
And if it seem evil unto you to serve the LORD, choose you this day whom ye will serve; whether the gods which your fathers served that were on the other side of the flood, or the gods of the Amorites, in whose land ye dwell: but as for me and my house, we will serve the LORD.

B. I have stuck unto thy testimonies
This is the very same Hebrew word as "cleaveth" above. When we are well grounded on the brevity of this life, we ought also be well fixed to the plan of God for life.

C. I will run the way of thy commandments
There won't be any hesitation. We ought to come to the place in our lives that we do what God says before the world, the flesh and the devil have any time to talk us out of it.

A REPEATED PRAYER
Psalms 119:25 (KJV)
... quicken thou me according to thy word.

Psalms 119:26 (KJV)
... teach me thy statutes.

Psalms 119:27 (KJV)
Make me to understand the way of thy precepts: ...

Psalms 119:28 (KJV)
... strengthen thou me according unto thy word.

Psalms 119:29 (KJV)
... and grant me thy law graciously.

I would like to remind all of us that the Christian life is a Spirit enabled life, or it is not a Christian life at all. You can do all the right things. But if it is not the Lord empowering those things, it's just clouds without rain – meaningless. To learn to pray, not **how to** pray **but to** pray is "faith 101."

Chapter Seven
HE is the FIRST CAUSE
Psalms 119:33-40 (KJV) HE

Teach me, O LORD, the way of thy statutes; and I shall keep it unto the end.

Give me understanding, and I shall keep thy law; yea, I shall observe it with my whole heart.

Make me to go in the path of thy commandments; for therein do I delight.

Incline my heart unto thy testimonies, and not to covetousness.

Turn away mine eyes from beholding vanity; and quicken thou me in thy way.

Stablish thy word unto thy servant, who is devoted to thy fear.

Turn away my reproach which I fear: for thy judgments are good.

Behold, I have longed after thy precepts: quicken me in thy righteousness.

I read that the fifth letter of the Hebrew alphabet, HE, is used at the beginning of verbs to make them causative. This stanza is a **prayer**. The Psalmist is pleading with God to cause him both

- **To understand God's Word and**
- **To obey God's Word**

Such understanding and obedience, which can only be gained through the hand of the Lord, causes a change in us. We become

- **Renewed**
- **Transformed**
- **Changed**

from the form of this world into a more Christlike person.

No wonder so many professing Christians are not much like Jesus.

- **They assume they understand the Word instead of begging God to cause them to know it.**
- **They assume they behave as Christians instead of begging God to cause them to obey it and therefore**

- **They only assume that they are Christlike instead of begging the Lord to cause them to be Christlike**

There are eight prayer requests in the stanza. I will divide them into three main classifications

A PRAYER FOR PERSPECTIVE
Understanding the Bible

A. Setting the stage
Psalms 119:33-34 (KJV)
Teach me, O LORD, the way of thy statutes; and I shall keep it unto the end.
Give me understanding, and I shall keep thy law; yea, I shall observe it with my whole heart.

Someone has suggested that the first two of these eight verses set the stage for everything else that is here.

Without a Holy Spirit understanding of the Word of God we are adrift. We're like a boat without power. We are afloat, but we are helpless to go wherever the tides and the currents take us. It is the Holy Spirit who turns what we learn in the Word of God into something that gives us power to go, often against the current to the destination God has for us.

We do not know the Bible just because:
- **We were taught the Bible in Sunday school**
- **Our parents told us what the Bible says God wants for us**
- **We've read the Bible in our daily devotions for years**

Experience has taught me that very few professing Christians have even read their Bible through.
A handful have maybe one time. Almost no one, except for some preachers, have ever obeyed.
2 Timothy 2:15 (KJV)

Study to shew thyself approved unto God, a workman that needeth not to be ashamed, rightly dividing the word of truth.

But even then, there is no power in that unless the Holy Spirit of God has illuminated the study.

B. Seeing what not to see
Psalms 119:37 (KJV)
Turn away mine eyes from beholding vanity; and quicken thou me in thy way.

At the same time God begins to remove the scales from our eyes so that we see what the Word of God says, another thing needs to happen, we need God's help to turn from what we have been looking at and thinking all our lives. I've seen it happen more often than I can count – including in myself. We obey what we learn in the Bible until we get under pressure. And then we do what we know.

Parents are notorious for it. Doesn't matter what the Bible says, without supernatural intervention, when push comes to shove, for good or for bad, we will raise our kids like our parents raised us.

A PRAYER FOR PRIORITIES
A focus on the Bible

A. Lean into it
Psalms 119:36 (KJV)
Incline my heart unto thy testimonies, and not to covetousness.

My wife loves sunflowers, so I attempt to grow some for her every year. Sunflowers are interesting to watch. Not only do they look a little bit like the sun and hence the name, but also, the flower follows the sun. The sunflower inclines its face toward the sun. That is what the Psalmist is praying in this verse. He's not simply asking that he do the right thing. He is asking God to give him an inclination, a bent; he is asking God to help him lean toward the Word of God.

And he is asking the Lord to help Him to lean toward His testimonies rather than to covetousness. That word means something that isn't mine. I can never have enough of the Word of God But I don't need any more of the things of this world than God is pleased to give me.

B. Long for it
Psalms 119:40 (KJV)
Behold, I have longed after thy precepts: quicken me in thy righteousness.

Longing for God's precepts is exactly the opposite of covetousness.

- **To covet is to have an undue, inordinate desire for what is not yours.**
- **To long for God's precepts is to have a thirst and hunger for what the sin nature stole from us.**

A PRAYER FOR PERFORMANCE
Obedience to the Bible

A. The Path of Obedience
Psalms 119:35 (KJV)
Make me to go in the path of thy commandments; for therein do I delight.

I have met a few Christians who take this passage in a very bad direction. They are just about to make a very bad choice, or at least a choice they suspect is not what God wants. But they know they should pray about it so their prayer goes something like this, "God, if you don't want me to do this thing, then make it so I can't do it." And then they will say something like, "God did not close the door, so it must be His will."

Notice that the Psalmist is praying about his path. There is a path for each of us in life. But this was "the path of thy commandments." He wasn't praying, "God show me where you want me to go." He was praying, "God lead me in a path that obeys your Word."

B. The path of fear
Psalms 119:38 (KJV)
Stablish thy word unto thy servant, who is devoted to thy fear.

People don't like to talk about the fear of God today. Christians tend to soften their version of the fear of the Lord. The Psalmist said he was "*devoted to thy fear*." And that fear, he prayed, would be used of the Lord to keep his feet firmly set where they belonged.

Chapter Eight
VAU, A CALL TO ACTION
Psalms 119:41-48 (KJV)
Let thy mercies come also unto me, O LORD, even thy salvation, according to thy word.
So shall I have wherewith to answer him that reproacheth me: for I trust in thy word.
And take not the word of truth utterly out of my mouth; for I have hoped in thy judgments.
So shall I keep thy law continually for ever and ever.
And I will walk at liberty: for I seek thy precepts.
I will speak of thy testimonies also before kings, and will not be ashamed.
And I will delight myself in thy commandments, which I have loved.
My hands also will I lift up unto thy commandments, which I have loved; and I will meditate in thy statutes.

Frequently certain religious traditions and customs become so engrained in our thinking that we apply them to Scripture without realizing we've done it. Verse forty-eight has a phrase that we might be guilty of doing that.

We tend to think of lifting up the hands as an act of worship. I think it is the idea of reaching up to God, trying to touch the Lord in our moment of worship. I don't think it is wrong.
Nehemiah 8:6 (KJV)
And Ezra blessed the LORD, the great God. And all the people answered, Amen, Amen, with lifting up their hands: and they bowed their heads, and worshipped the LORD with their faces to the ground.

But that is not the only way we use our hands, is it? Our hands are a symbol of our work.
Ephesians 4:28 (KJV)
Let him that stole steal no more: but rather let him labour, working with his hands the thing which is good, that he may have to give to him that needeth.

It seems to me that this is a more appropriate application of Psalms 119:48. It does very little benefit to read the Bible, hear the Bible preached, or memorize parts of the Bible and then just look up to God, stretch out our hands and say, "Praise the Lord, I really love that!" The thing to do with the Word of God is to do the Word of God. We ought to see the Bible as a call to action, and so, when we are given the Word of God, act upon it.

AN ACTIVE FAITH
Psalms 119:41-42 (KJV)
Let thy mercies come also unto me, O LORD, even thy salvation, according to thy word.
So shall I have wherewith to answer him that reproacheth me: for I trust in thy word.

I want to key in just a moment on the word, "trust." This and the next point contain Christian terms that we recognize, but I am not sure we know how to "do."

Trust. The idea is that of leaning on, finding support in. How do we lean on and trust God's Word.

Think of David. He had the promise that he would be king after Saul. Almost immediately after hearing that promise from the preacher, Samuel, his world fell apart. Everything about his circumstances told him that God's promise wasn't going to happen.

How did he demonstrate a trust in the Word of God?
- **He waited faithfully upon the Lord**
- **He didn't take matters in his own hands**
- **He didn't fall into despair**

God gave him a hand full of people to lead and he led them until God did something else. An active faith waits on the Lord

AN ACTIVE HOPE

Psalms 119:43 (KJV)

And take not the word of truth utterly out of my mouth; for I have hoped in thy judgments.

If faith is leaning, hope is looking.

Titus 2:13 (KJV)

Looking for that blessed hope, and the glorious appearing of the great God and our Saviour Jesus Christ;

I imagine everyone who has been in the military understands how looking can be a very active duty.

I watched a video of a situation involving a police officer in California. Several officers had been called in to deal with a man threatening people with a gun. One officer was stationed at the corner of a building in case the guy came that way. But the situation took a long time to play out and eventually this particular office pulled out a couple of milk crates and sit down on them. Wouldn't you know it, this guy, who has been threatening to shoot policemen, but who almost certainly wasn't going to come around by this officer, comes running around the corner.

The officer, shocked, stands up, backs up and trips over the crates he had been sitting on. Fortunately, he was able to compose himself well enough that, while still sitting on the ground after tripping, could shoot the bad guy before he got shot. Sitting down looking at the ground, in his case, wasn't watching. Watching would have been expecting that, at any moment, the guy was going to come around his way.

1 Peter 5:8 (KJV)

Be sober, be vigilant; because your adversary the devil, as a roaring lion, walketh about, seeking whom he may devour:

Those are negative illustrations of hope but the positive is,
Mark 13:35 (KJV)
Watch ye therefore: for ye know not when the master of the house
cometh, at even, or at midnight, or at the cockcrowing, or in the
morning:

Hope is to actively watch for the Lord to come again.

AN ACTIVE WALK
Psalms 119:44-45 (KJV)
So shall I keep thy law continually for ever and ever.
And I will walk at liberty: for I seek thy precepts.

I am interested in the contrast in these verses between law
and liberty. So many ear tickling Christians these days
gloat in what they call liberty. There was Mark Driscoll up
in the Seattle area who gloated about his liberty in Christ.
He said he was preaching the Bible straight but that he
wouldn't put any legalistic restrictions on the people in his
church – and he did gather a huge bunch, for a while.
- **They had classes on beer making**
- **They got together to smoke cigars and talk Bible**
- **They had men's activities where they went out and got tattoos together**

I even think he might have been one of those guys who put
a bed on the roof of the church so that he and his wife could
lie there and teach couples how to have a good marriage.

But after a little bit people thought even he was too strict.
Today his huge buildings sit empty.
And he has some insignificant internet teaching ministry.

The Bible teaches that true freedom COMES from
submission to the commandments of God's Word.

AN ACTIVE TESTIMONY
Psalms 119:46-47 (KJV)

I will speak of thy testimonies also before kings, and will not be ashamed.
And I will delight myself in thy commandments, which I have loved.

I see three activities in these two verses:

A. Speak

I can't see any way to get around the fact that the Bible teaches us to talk about the Bible. "True witnessing is not the sharing of a personal experience—true witnessing is the communication of the word of God. Sharing is subjective; witnessing is objective. Sharing flows from the heart of man; witnessing flows from the heart of God."[17]

Witnessing is not giving your own opinions and experience about being a Christian. It is telling people what the Word of God says.

B. Boldness

The Psalmist said he would speak the Word of God to kings. I imagine that means he would speak it to everyone else too.

Boldness isn't brashness, rudeness or even confidence. Boldness stems from trust. It's just doing it anyway. Speaking the Word of God is what God wants us to do, so we do it.

C. Delight

We must delight in God's commandments in order to speak it boldly.

The word "delight" has to do with loving it, embracing it, watching over it. The Hebrew word comes from one that means to devour. When we consume the Word of God, it becomes much easier to speak the Word boldly.

---

[17] Word of Truth PDF on a witness

AN ACTIVE MEDITATION
Psalms 119:48 (KJV)
My hands also will I lift up unto thy commandments, which I have loved; and I will meditate in thy statutes.

I have three Hebrew dictionaries I use to help in my studies. Brown-Driver-Briggs gives as it FIRST definition of meditate, "to put forth" as in "to put forth and effort. Thinking about the Bible, learning it is an active effort.

I had a conversation with a man who asked me to help him find some Bible verses to bring him out of depression. I've never given this counsel in a situation like this before, but I think it is the best counsel. I told him to start reading his Bible and not to stop until the Holy Spirit showed him some verses to bring him out of his depression.

The Bible isn't a pill that we take two of and then everything is better. It is a diet that we consume some of every day, several times a day, so that it nourishes and strengthen our soul a spirit and we become what it gives us.

Chapter Nine

THIS I HAD

Psalms 119:49-56 (KJV) **ZAIN**
Remember the word unto thy servant, upon which thou hast caused me to hope.
This is my comfort in my affliction: for thy word hath quickened me.
The proud have had me greatly in derision: yet have I not declined from thy law.
I remembered thy judgments of old, O LORD; and have comforted myself.
Horror hath taken hold upon me because of the wicked that forsake thy law.
Thy statutes have been my songs in the house of my pilgrimage.
I have remembered thy name, O LORD, in the night, and have kept thy law.
This I had, because I kept thy precepts.

There is, in the faith of the Christian, a mysterious duality that can be very very difficult to describe to someone who is not experiencing it with you.

On the one hand, the Bible says that we are to *"rejoice evermore"*[18] but at the same time the Bible says, *"Blessed are they that mourn."*[19]
On the one hand the Bible says, *"greater is He that is in you than He that is in the world"*[20] but on the other hand the Bible says, *"Behold I send you forth and sheep in the midst of wolves."*[21]

---

[18] 1 Thessalonians 5:16 (KJV)
Rejoice evermore.
[19] Matthew 5:4 (KJV)
Blessed are they that mourn: for they shall be comforted.
[20] 1 John 4:4 (KJV)
Ye are of God, little children, and have overcome them: because greater is he that is in you, than he that is in the world.
[21] Matthew 10:16 (KJV)
Behold, I send you forth as sheep in the midst of wolves: be ye therefore wise as serpents, and harmless as doves.

On the one hand the Bible says, *"so run that ye may obtain"*[22] but on the other hand the Bible says *"the first shall be last and the last shall be first."*[23]

God promises Christians can live a victorious life[24] but He has also called us to live a hard life.[25]

We don't get to choose for ourselves the life we want to live. We are called to a life of obedience to the Bible, no matter how difficult or uncomfortable that may be.

THE PSALMIST, DAVID, PRESENTS TO US SOME VERY DIFFICULT THINGS

Affliction
Psalms 119:50 (KJV)
This is my comfort in my affliction: for thy word hath quickened me.

It means "to furrow the eyebrow"
There is depression and oppression –

Derision
Psalms 119:51 (KJV)
The proud have had me greatly in derision: yet have I not declined from thy law.

---

[22] 1 Corinthians 9:24 (KJV)
Know ye not that they which run in a race run all, but one receiveth the prize? So run, that ye may obtain.
[23] Matthew 20:16 (KJV)
So the last shall be first, and the first last: for many be called, but few chosen.
[24] 1 Corinthians 15:57 (KJV)
But thanks be to God, which giveth us the victory through our Lord Jesus Christ.
[25] 2 Timothy 2:3 (KJV)
Thou therefore endure hardness, as a good soldier of Jesus Christ.

This is the idea of mocking, laughing at us in contempt.
The Bible says this is "great derision."

Horror
Psalms 119:53 (KJV)
Horror hath taken hold upon me because of the wicked that forsake thy law.

This is a trembling anger. You become terrified.

Pilgrimage
Psalms 119:54 (KJV)
Thy statutes have been my songs in the house of my pilgrimage.

This carries with it the idea of homelessness.
Abraham gave up his home to obey God. He never felt at home again on this earth.

He chose instead to wait for God to give him the one God would make for him.[26]

When Abraham went to Egypt it was an attempt on his part to choose for himself a place not where God had put him.

Notice, he did not go back to the Ur of Chaldees, but he didn't want to stay where God had placed him.

Nowhere does the Bible describe the Christian life as one of comfort, ease and gratification.

---

[26] Hebrews 11:9-10 (KJV)
By faith he sojourned in the land of promise, as in a strange country, dwelling in tabernacles with Isaac and Jacob, the heirs with him of the same promise:
For he looked for a city which hath foundations, whose builder and maker is God.

God puts us in a dark place, where we do not feel at home.

But then, notice that God does not leave us there without help.

THE PSALMIST, DAVID, THEN DESCRIBES WHAT GOD GAVE HIM TO HELP HIM THROUGH THE HARDNESS

God gave him hope
Psalms 119:49 (KJV)
Remember the word unto thy servant, upon which thou hast caused me to hope.
The word hope means, "a confident expectation."

I have some friends, men I love dearly, who teach that it is unhealthy to have expectations. They believe that when you have expectations, you are just setting yourself up or pain.

So
They place no expectations on their children
And their children are not properly disciplined.

They place no expectations in their relationships
So that they can't get hurt when someone leaves them.

Ultimately
They place no expectations upon themselves
So they are not disappointed if they fail at what they do.

The Bible teaches us that those who have no hope are without Christ.

- **Because of Christ we can expect that our children can grow up in the nurture and the admonition of the Lord**

- **Because of Christ we can expect that we can have healthy relationships both in our marriage and at church**
- **Because of Christ we can expect that God will use us in ways we would never have imagined.**

The Psalmist said he had hope.

God gave him Comfort
Psalms 119:50 (KJV)
This is my comfort in my affliction: for thy word hath quickened me.

The word comfort has to do with **consolation**. It's a gift or prize to encourage you when you are down.

I think the best way to understand it is in the word "**quickened**." Whenever we are afflicted, in any trouble, God gives us what we need to **sustain our life**.

God gave him Songs
Psalms 119:54 (KJV)
Thy statutes have been my songs in the house of my pilgrimage.

The devil has almost ruined Christian music today.
So much of it is shallow and meaningless that it has lost much of its value.

Think about
- **"A mighty fortress is our God, a bulwark never failing."**
- **"Stand up, stand up or Jesus, ye soldiers of the cross"**
- **"It is well, it is well, with my soul"**
- **"Have thine own way Lord, have thine own way"**

It used to be, and I am convinced it still would work, that hymns could be prescribed as a means of those with illness related to the spirit, soul, and mind.

Instead of going to a therapist, or a counselor or a psychiatrist a Christian would be much better served by listening to the right songs.

- **Some can encourage**
- **Some can correct**
- **Some can challenge if they are the right ones**

They can all instruct.

The Psalmist didn't deny the trouble in his life. I am certain that the person who does not have to battle to be where God wants him to be, has something wrong with them spiritually.

But the Christian who is in the battle for the Lord has some God given help
Hope
Comfort and
Songs

But notice he says, Psalms 119:56 (KJV)
This I had, because I kept thy precepts.

Not because he knew them
- **Not because he believed them**
- **Not because he agreed with them**
- **Not even because he had taught them**

Because he kept, he obeyed, he practiced the Word of God.

Can you see the difference between agreeing that this is the Word of God and actually doing what the Bible says?

Can you say before God that you are a doer of His Word, not just a hearer?

Chapter Ten

MY PORTION
A Sermon in a Stanza

Psalms 119:57-64 (KJV) CHETH

Thou art my portion, O LORD: I have said that I would keep thy words.
I intreated thy favour with my whole heart: be merciful unto me according to thy word.
I thought on my ways, and turned my feet unto thy testimonies.
I made haste, and delayed not to keep thy commandments.
The bands of the wicked have robbed me: but I have not forgotten thy law.
At midnight I will rise to give thanks unto thee because of thy righteous judgments.
I am a companion of all them that fear thee, and of them that keep thy precepts.
The earth, O LORD, is full of thy mercy: teach me thy statutes.

We come this morning to consider the ninth of the twenty-two stanzas of Psalms 119, each corresponding to the letters of the Hebrew Alphabet

This stanza is organized in much the same way a preacher would organize a sermon
There is an introduction
Which is often a summary of what the message will attempt to deliver.
There is the body
Which attempts to lay out in order the points of the message so that they resonate with the congregation.
There is the call
Which is an appeal to respond to the message of the sermon in some positive way relating to our walk with the Lord

THE INTRODUCTION
Psalms 119:57 (KJV)

Thou art my portion, O LORD: I have said that I would keep thy words.

Notice the phrase
A. *"Thou art my portion, O LORD."*

The word, portion, means
- **Your share**
- **Your award**
- **Your possession**
- **Your parcel of land**

The word is found 114 times in the Old Testament.

The allusion takes us to the land of Israel divided among the tribes. Each tribe receives its own portion which we might almost look at as individual state.

Every tribe got their own portion, except the tribe of Levi because the Lord was their portion.

It doesn't mean that they didn't have any land or places to live. Each of the other tribes, divided out a part of their portion and gave them to the Levites so that the Levites lived among all of the tribes.

The idea that was being taught was that God's people live among the people of the world, but their inheritance, the thing they lived for, is the Lord.

Think about the priests for a moment
- **They had homes**
- **They had fields**
- **They had crops to plant and harvest**
- **They had families**
- **They had cities**

But they were not to view any of those things as the portion God had given them.

They belonged to God and He belonged to them.

I want to ask you how true would that be of you?

Is it even a desire to which you hope to attain?

None of us are perfect, but if we do not have a target at which to shoot, or if we have the wrong target, how can we ever hope to grow in grace and the knowledge of the Lord?

This desire is the motivation for the second phrase,
B. *"I have said that I would keep thy words"*
Unless we view the Lord, and not something in this world, as our portion, we have no compelling reason to keep the Words of the Bible.

THE BODY
Psalms 119:58-63 (KJV)
I intreated thy favour with my whole heart: be merciful unto me according to thy word.
I thought on my ways, and turned my feet unto thy testimonies.
I made haste, and delayed not to keep thy commandments.
The bands of the wicked have robbed me: but I have not forgotten thy law.
At midnight I will rise to give thanks unto thee because of thy righteous judgments.
I am a companion of all them that fear thee, and of them that keep thy precepts.

The Lord is my portion – He is my award – He is my everything.

Because of that I want to keep and obey His word.

But I know that I can say I will God's Word all day long. It won't happen without planning.

A. I need the to rely on the mercy promised in the Word of God

Psalms 119:58 (KJV)

I intreated thy favour with my whole heart: be merciful unto me according to thy word.

B. I need to choose a way that is obedient to God's Word

Psalms 119:59 (KJV)

I thought on my ways, and turned my feet unto thy testimonies.

C. I need to develop an attitude that is obedient to God's Word

Psalms 119:60-62 (KJV)

I made haste, and delayed not to keep thy commandments.
The bands of the wicked have robbed me: but I have not forgotten thy law.
At midnight I will rise to give thanks unto thee because of thy righteous judgments.

D. I need to have friends who want to be obedient to God's Word.

Psalms 119:63 (KJV)

I am a companion of all them that fear thee, and of them that keep thy precepts.

THE FINAL CALL

Psalms 119:64 (KJV)

The earth, O LORD, is full of thy mercy: teach me thy statutes.

All that was before this verse was affirmation of doctrine and application of truth.

- **"This is what the Bible says" and**
- **"This is what I will do"**

At this point the Psalmist gets real with Himself and prays.

In the end, Lord, all I have is Your mercy.
I pray that YOU, LORD, teach me....

Too much Christianity today is ready made and in the bag.
- **I prayed for salvation and received it**
- **I joined a church and attend it**
- **I have my ministry and do it**

It's all good.
Nothing to be concerned about.

Not so the Psalmist.
"All I have LORD, is Your mercy.
Teach me thy statutes."

Chapter Eleven
GOD HAS BEEN GOOD

Psalms 119:65-72 (KJV) **TETH**

Thou hast dealt well with thy servant, O LORD, according unto thy word.

Teach me good judgment and knowledge: for I have believed thy commandments.

Before I was afflicted I went astray: but now have I kept thy word.

Thou art good, and doest good; teach me thy statutes.

The proud have forged a lie against me: but I will keep thy precepts with my whole heart.

Their heart is as fat as grease; but I delight in thy law.

It is good for me that I have been afflicted; that I might learn thy statutes.

The law of thy mouth is better unto me than thousands of gold and silver.

We come this morning to the ninth of the twenty-two stanzas of Psalms 119.

For those who may have not been here, or may not remember, this Psalm is the longest "chapter" in all of the Bible.

- **It is almost exactly in the middle of the Bible.**
- **It has 176 verses in all.[27] The remarkable thing is**
- **In contains something about the Bible in every verse, except one.[28]**

---

[27] In most cases that would not matter much because the chapters and verses were added many years after the books of the Bible were written. They were added primarily to aide in study and expounding of the Word of God. In this case, however, the structure is clearly laid out. Each stanza corresponds to one of the letters of the Hebrew alphabet. Each line of the stanza – eight in everyone -begins with the corresponding letter.

[28] Psalms 119:122 (KJV)

Be surety for thy servant for good: let not the proud oppress me.

An obvious lesson is JUST HOW IMPORTANT THE BIBLE IS TO OUR FAITH.

Being a serious student of the Bible is not mandatory to be saved.
- **But walking in the Spirit**
- **Following the Lord**
- **Doing His will**

All require something much greater than just the assumption that you know the Bible because you've gone to church your whole life.

Consider

2 Timothy 2:15 (KJV)

Study to shew thyself approved unto God, a workman that needeth not to be ashamed, rightly dividing the word of truth.

A sure way to be ashamed when you stand before the Lord, is to behave in a manner you assume is right, but is not guided by the Word of God.

The stanza we have before us has three obvious themes –
- **a greater one and**
- **a lesser one and**
- **an even lesser one**

The greater one – God has been good – is found five times.[29]

---

[29] Psalms 119:65 (KJV)

Thou hast dealt well with thy servant, O LORD, according unto thy word.

Psalms 119:66 (KJV)

Teach me good judgment and knowledge: for I have believed thy commandments.

Psalms 119:68 (KJV)

Thou art good, and doest good; teach me thy statutes.

Psalms 119:71 (KJV)

It is good for me that I have been afflicted; that I might learn thy statutes.

Psalms 119:72 (KJV)

The lesser one- teach me – is found three times.[30]
The lesser one – in affliction – is found twice.[31]

God has dealt well with us
AS HIS WORD HAS SAID HE WOULD
Psalms 119:65 (KJV)
Thou hast dealt well with thy servant, O LORD, according unto thy word.

The Psalmist boldly claims the God had been good to Him exactly as He said He would.

Listen – God is good.
God intends good for us.
Jeremiah 29:11 (KJV)
For I know the thoughts that I think toward you, saith the LORD, thoughts of peace, and not of evil, to give you an expected end.

Romans 8:28 (KJV)
And we know that all things work together for good to them that love God, to them who are the called according to his purpose.

- **This does not mean that everything that happens in the life of a Christian is good.**

The law of thy mouth is better unto me than thousands of gold and silver.
[30] Psalms 119:66 (KJV)
Teach me good judgment and knowledge: for I have believed thy commandments.
Psalms 119:68 (KJV)
Thou art good, and doest good; teach me thy statutes.
Psalms 119:71 (KJV)
It is good for me that I have been afflicted; that I might learn thy statutes.
[31] Psalms 119:67 (KJV)
Before I was afflicted I went astray: but now have I kept thy word.
Psalms 119:71 (KJV)
It is good for me that I have been afflicted; that I might learn thy statutes.

- **It does mean that God intends good for us.**

According to His Word also means that it is the kind of good that is defined in the Bible and not the kind of good that men have decided for themselves.

People think that things are good that clearly are not.
God is under no obligation to honor our own understanding of good and evil.

But He has dealt well with us according to His Word.

God has dealt well with us
BY TEACHING US HIS WORD
Psalms 119:66-71 (KJV)
Teach me good judgment and knowledge: for I have believed thy commandments.
Before I was afflicted I went astray: but now have I kept thy word.
Thou art good, and doest good; teach me thy statutes.
The proud have forged a lie against me: but I will keep thy precepts with my whole heart.
Their heart is as fat as grease; but I delight in thy law.
It is good for me that I have been afflicted; that I might learn thy statutes.

God teaches us
A. Through faith
Psalms 119:66 (KJV)
Teach me good judgment and knowledge: for I have believed thy commandments.

A person who does not believe the Bible simply will not understand the Bible.
They are blinded through unbelief.[32]

---

[32] 2 Corinthians 4:4 (KJV)
In whom the god of this world hath blinded the minds of them which believe not, lest the light of the glorious gospel of Christ, who is the

God teaches us
B. Despite liars
Psalms 119:69 (KJV)
The proud have forged a lie against me: but I will keep thy precepts with my whole heart.

Those who do not believe the Bible, cannot understand the Bible. Neither do they understand those who do believe the Bible.

So, they lie about us.
- **They call us hate-mongers**
- **They insist that all the bad things in the world are the result of our faith**
- **They accuse of us being mean spirited of attacking them**

when, in fact, we only tell them what the Bible says.

God teaches us
C. In affliction
Psalms 119:71 (KJV)
It is good for me that I have been afflicted; that I might learn thy statutes.

This may be the hardest lesson to learn but we're not really learning anything spiritually while everything is going our way.

It takes affliction to separate our heart from the world and truly look to heaven.

God has dealt well with us
IN GIVING US HIS WORD
Psalms 119:72 (KJV)
The law of thy mouth is better unto me than thousands of gold and silver.

---

image of God, should shine unto them.

- **If you have the Bible**
- **If you have a heart to learn the Bible**
- **If you have come to the place where you would rather obey the Bible than have anything in the world**

Then you are among the wealthiest people in the world.[33]

---

[33] Mark 8:35-36 (KJV)

For whosoever will save his life shall lose it; but whosoever shall lose his life for my sake and the gospel's, the same shall save it.
For what shall it profit a man, if he shall gain the whole world, and lose his own soul?

Chapter Twelve

THAT I

Psalms 119:73-80 (KJV) JOD

Thy hands have made me and fashioned me: give me understanding, that I may learn thy commandments.
They that fear thee will be glad when they see me; because I have hoped in thy word.
I know, O LORD, that thy judgments are right, and that thou in faithfulness hast afflicted me.
Let, I pray thee, thy merciful kindness be for my comfort, according to thy word unto thy servant.
Let thy tender mercies come unto me, that I may live: for thy law is my delight.
Let the proud be ashamed; for they dealt perversely with me without a cause: but I will meditate in thy precepts.
Let those that fear thee turn unto me, and those that have known thy testimonies.
Let my heart be sound in thy statutes; that I be not ashamed.

I notice in this tenth stanza three sort of "conditional" statements:

That I may learn
Vs 73
That I am live
Vs 77
That I be not ashamed
Vs 80

The psalmist knows he is a needy man.

- **He does not know all he needs to know or ought to know.**
- **His life is but a vapor, so he must prepare for eternity and**
- **He will give an account before the Lord one day**

The Bible is the answer for each of these needs.

FOUNDATIONAL REALITY

There are two realities that form the basis for the truths presented and their ability to meet our needs.

You realize, as I do, that it is not everyone who finds the Bible to be that helpful.

I've been meditating lately on three things I absolutely know are true and how those three things serve to sustain me.
- **I know God is**
- **I know the Bible is His Word to me and**
- **I know believers are to be committed to the local church God fitted them for**

Armed with those truths I wake up each morning to serve the Lord.

The Psalmist declares some assumptions that serve the same purpose for him.

A. God made and fashioned us
Psalms 119:73 (KJV)
Thy hands have made me and fashioned me: give me understanding, that I may learn thy commandments.

This is a basis for all that is true.
- **God is**
- **God made us**

The Bible starts out Genesis 1:1 (KJV)
In the beginning God created the heaven and the earth.

The reason why creation is such an important truth, and the reason why the unbelieving world attacks it so viciously is because if you do not believe Genesis 1:1 nothing else in the Bible matters.

The psalmist says
Thy hands have made me and fashioned me.

I am therefore responsible to Him.

And then He says
B. God's judgments are right
Psalms 119:75 (KJV)
I know, O LORD, that thy judgments are right, and that thou in faithfulness hast afflicted me.

I know.

I know.

I know this for a fact – that they judgments are right.

Every Word of God – even those that denounce our sins and lead to the chastening of them is right.

Notice that the context is *"that thou in faithfulness hast afflicted me."*

I know that to be true. In the middle of a season of difficulty and affliction, God is still right, and God is still faithful.

FUNDAMENTAL REACTION
God, being who God is and we being who we are, the appropriate reaction to everything is prayer.

A. Prayer for understanding
Psalms 119:73 (KJV)
... give me understanding, that I may learn thy commandments.

I need God to help me learn His right judgments with my affliction.

B. Prayer for comfort

Psalms 119:76-77 (KJV)
Let, I pray thee, thy merciful kindness be for my comfort, according to thy word unto thy servant.
Let thy tender mercies come unto me, that I may live: for thy law is my delight.

Given that we are afflicted, Lord we ask you for your merciful kindness and your comfort.

C. Prayer for companionship
Psalms 119:79 (KJV)
Let those that fear thee turn unto me, and those that have known thy testimonies.

This is what a church is.
It's a group of people who
- **fear the Lord together,**
- **understand God's Word together and**
- **seek God's mercy together**

D. Prayer for soundness
Psalms 119:80 (KJV)
Let my heart be sound in thy statutes; that I be not ashamed.

Soundness means whole, complete, mature.

A horse that is "sound" is completely healthy.
- **His feet**
- **His legs**
- **His hips**
- **His mouth**
- **His conformation**

We ought to be praying that every part of us be conformed to the image of Jesus Christ.

FRIENDLY RESPONSE

A. Gladness

Psalms 119:74 (KJV)
They that fear thee will be glad when they see me; because I have hoped in thy word.

The opposite of being ashamed is to be glad.

Not a giddy "up one minute and down the next" sentiment, but the ability to look another believer in the eye and to come boldly to the throne of grace.

Where the cycle repeats with prayer again.

Chapter Thirteen
DESPERATE TIMES
Psalms 119:81-88 (KJV) CAPH.

My soul fainteth for thy salvation: but I hope in thy word.
Mine eyes fail for thy word, saying, When wilt thou comfort me?
For I am become like a bottle in the smoke; yet do I not forget thy statutes.
How many are the days of thy servant? when wilt thou execute judgment on them that persecute me?
The proud have digged pits for me, which are not after thy law.
All thy commandments are faithful: they persecute me wrongfully; help thou me.
They had almost consumed me upon earth; but I forsook not thy precepts.
Quicken me after thy lovingkindness; so shall I keep the testimony of thy mouth.

I've recently begun trying to broadcast my daily devotions in a podcast format. I started with the book of Proverbs, one of the most helpful books I think we have in the Bible.

Of course, these have been written, some of them, many years ago. I am blessed that the Word of God, which blessed me twenty years ago, can still bless me today. I recorded one of them this last week from Proverbs 3:5-6 on the subject of trust.

I illustrated trust from my old apprentice ironworker days working on what we called a rebar curtain. It was a wall of rebar tied together. The crew I was on would carry a length of rebar, maybe 30 feet long, climbing the curtain like you would a ladder. When we got to where were would tie the rebar, we would "hook off" with a snap hook built into our built, then we would lean back on the hook allowing it to take our weight and freeing our hands to work.

The first few times you hook off is terrifying. Then, when you lean back – remember there were maybe five men leaning back at the same time, the curtain would begin to sway back and forth 5 or 6 feet each way. I was sure it would collapse backward, and we'd all fall to our deaths.

After a few times, though, you figure out that it isn't going to fall, and you can trust your life to it.

I bet that if I were to climb and hook off a rebar curtain today, I'd be just as frightened as the first time I did it. Though I know it is safe to do in my head, I haven't kept up my "faith."

The same thing happens to a Christian.
We learn early on we can trust the Lord.
But there can come the point in our Christian life when, if we haven't had to step out in faith very much, we panic at the thought of trusting God.

Though we know we can trust Him; we're not sure we want to.

That is where the Psalmist is at about this point in our text.

The Psalm breaks easily into two parts:
A Cry of Desperation and
A Call of Deliverance

A CRY OF DESPERATION
Psalms 119:81-82 (KJV)
My soul fainteth for thy salvation: but I hope in thy word.
Mine eyes fail for thy word, saying, When wilt thou comfort me?

A. Desperation of his soul
Vs. 81

He admits that his soul "fainteth."

- **He feels like he has taken about all the abuse he can.**
- **He feels like giving up**
- **He feels, maybe not like quitting, but for sure like dying.**[34]

I say not quitting because he also says. *"but I hope in thy Word."*

The Bible can lift up the weary and restore hope in him.

- **He's at the end of his rope.**
- **But he still has his Bible.**

B. The desperation of his eyes
Vs. 82
Mine eyes fail for thy word, saying, When wilt thou comfort me?

This was a desperate time when he was so faint that he had difficulty focusing on the Word of God.

**"When God, when?
I hope in thy Word. I have hoped for so long."**

"When Lord, when wilt thou finally comfort me?"

He's desperate.

I want to encourage you to be faithful and consistent in finding health in the Bible because, when you are desperate, when you are at the end of your rope, it's going to be very hard to start then.

---

[34] Many of the Old Testament saints spoke about how they would just like for the battle to be over – they wished they could die.

Like a starving person, he can't be fed right away once rescued. His system would not receive it.

Sometimes a starving person starves to death even when food is in front of them because they are too far gone to take it in.

A CALL FOR DELIVERANCE
Psalms 119:83-88 (KJV)
For I am become like a bottle in the smoke; yet do I not forget thy statutes.
How many are the days of thy servant? when wilt thou execute judgment on them that persecute me?
The proud have digged pits for me, which are not after thy law.
All thy commandments are faithful: they persecute me wrongfully; help thou me.
They had almost consumed me upon earth; but I forsook not thy precepts.
Quicken me after thy lovingkindness; so shall I keep the testimony of thy mouth.

Deliver me
A. Because I am lonely and forgotten
Psalms 119:83 (KJV)
For I am become like a bottle in the smoke; yet do I not forget thy statutes.

Remember houses of that time were all heated by rudimentary fireplaces. They always had smoke in them.

Food stuffs and other things were stored in bottles and vessels on shelves and – if they were left a long time, would become discolored by the smoke in the room.

"A bottle in the smoke" was something forgotten and uncared for.

Ever felt like that?

But while he said he felt forgotten, he was not forgetful. *"yet do I not forget thy statutes."*

Deliver me
B. Because my life is short
Psalms 119:84 (KJV)
How many are the days of thy servant? when wilt thou execute judgment on them that persecute me?

The Bible has numerous passages urging us to take into account that our life his short.
- **It is a vapor**
- **It is as water spilt on the ground**
- **Etc.**

We are taught to number our days so that we apply our hearts to the wisdom of God's Word.

Another advantage of remembering the brevity of life is that we learn to be more patient concerning God's judgment.

It will happen sooner than they expect and soon enough for us.

Deliver me
C. Because I am innocent
Psalms 119:85-88 (KJV)
The proud have digged pits for me, which are not after thy law.
All thy commandments are faithful: they persecute me wrongfully; help thou me.
They had almost consumed me upon earth; but I forsook not thy precepts.
Quicken me after thy lovingkindness; so shall I keep the testimony of thy mouth.

None of us are innocent before God.

But the Christian is justified in Christ.

The Psalmist claims:
- **They have dug illegal pits for him**
- **They persecuted him wrongfully**
- **They had almost consumed him**

The Bible makes it clear that we can expect this sort of treatment in the world.
1 Peter 4:12-15 (KJV)

Beloved, think it not strange concerning the fiery trial which is to try you, as though some strange thing happened unto you:
But rejoice, inasmuch as ye are partakers of Christ's sufferings; that, when his glory shall be revealed, ye may be glad also with exceeding joy.
If ye be reproached for the name of Christ, happy are ye; for the spirit of glory and of God resteth upon you: on their part he is evil spoken of, but on your part he is glorified.
But let none of you suffer as a murderer, or as a thief, or as an evildoer, or as a busybody in other men's matters.

He was none of those evil things.

"but I forsook not thy precepts.
Quicken me after thy lovingkindness; so shall I keep the testimony of thy mouth."

Chapter Fourteen

FOR EVER

Psalms 119:89-96 (KJV) LAMED

For ever, O LORD, thy word is settled in heaven.
Thy faithfulness is unto all generations: thou hast established the earth, and it abideth.
They continue this day according to thine ordinances: for all are thy servants.
Unless thy law had been my delights, I should then have perished in mine affliction.
I will never forget thy precepts: for with them thou hast quickened me.
I am thine, save me; for I have sought thy precepts.
The wicked have waited for me to destroy me: but I will consider thy testimonies.
I have seen an end of all perfection: but thy commandment is exceeding broad.

This is the twelfth of 22 stanzas in the 119th Psalm.
- **Each stanza is built around one of the 22 letters of the Hebrew alphabet**
- **Each stanza contains 8 verses and**
- **Every verse, 176 in all, except one, contain some reference to the Word of God.**

The Bible
- **is our bread**
- **It is our milk**
- **It is our meat**

- **The Bible**
- **is sword**
- **It is our hammer**
- **It is our lamp to light our way**

The Bible is more than the tool we use for church services, 1 Corinthians 10:31 (KJV)
Whether therefore ye eat, or drink, or whatsoever ye do, do all to the glory of God.

What part of life would not be covered by *"whatsoever ye do"*?

We will not glorify God in anything whatsoever unless we do it in obedience to and following the guiding of the Bible.

Our Psalmist is settled on the Scriptures. And he's willing to say so.

A DECLARATION OF FAITH concerning the Word of God

Psalms 119:89-91 (KJV)

For ever, O LORD, thy word is settled in heaven.
Thy faithfulness is unto all generations: thou hast established the earth, and it abideth.
They continue this day according to thine ordinances: for all are thy servants.

The Bible is as unchanging as God is.

- He is the Rock upon which we build our house (church)
- He is the same yesterday today and forever
- He is the Lord, He changes not[35]

And what is true of God is equally true of the Bible.

It is settled.
- It is settled about spiritual matters
- It is settled about financial matters
- It is settled about civil and political matters
- It is settled about moral matters
- It is settled about sexual matters
- It is settled about matter of judgment

---

[35] Malachi 3:6 (KJV)

For I am the LORD, I change not; therefore ye sons of Jacob are not consumed.

- **It is settled about matters of eternity**

Here's the thing.
People who change the Bible, or believe the Bible can be changed, do so because they believe God can be changed. (They really do not believe in any god other than self.)

People who believe that we should change how we interpret the Bible to fit better into how real life is today do that because they do not believe in an unchanging God.

I believe in an eternal, all powerful, all knowing, and all present God.

Because of that, I believe this Bible is without error, needs no corrections, updates, or cultural tweaks.

I believe it does on fact contain all things that pertain to life and godliness.

I believe we ought to follow it,
- **Without question**
- **Without hesitation**

A DECLARATION OF FAITH concerning himself

Psalms 119:92-93 (KJV)
Unless thy law had been my delights, I should then have perished in mine affliction.
I will never forget thy precepts: for with them thou hast quickened me.

The Word of God is settled.
Like God, it never changes. We can build our life upon it.

That is not true of me and you.
- **We are often in affliction and suffering**

- We are easily consumed and given to perishing and
- We have but a brief stay on this planet

The Bible is like a rock that never changes.
We are like sand that is constantly shifting.

God builds in us stability when
- We delight in His law and
- Never forget His precepts

The two are complimentary.
We would never remember the Word of God if we did not at first delight in or love the Word of God.

A DECLARATION OF FAITH concerning God

Psalms 119:94-96 (KJV)
I am thine, save me; for I have sought thy precepts.
The wicked have waited for me to destroy me: but I will consider thy testimonies.
I have seen an end of all perfection: but thy commandment is exceeding broad.

These three verses are amazing. They describe to us the whole process of redemption.

A. Salvation

Psalms 119:94 (KJV)
I am thine, save me; for I have sought thy precepts.
Salvation of our soul happens the moment we trust our keeping to Christ.

At that moment we are bought.
We are not our own.[36]

---

[36] 1 Corinthians 6:19-20 (KJV)
What? know ye not that your body is the temple of the Holy Ghost which is in you, which ye have of God, and ye are not your own?

And that happens to us through the Word of God.

Romans 10:17 (KJV)
So then faith cometh by hearing, and hearing by the word of God.

B. Deliverance
Psalms 119:95 (KJV)
The wicked have waited for me to destroy me: but I will consider thy testimonies.

Having been saved, we discover that we have been enlisted into the Lord's army.
- **We have enemies.[37]**
- **We endure hardness and good soldiers[38] and**
- **We pray to the to be delivered from all evil[39]**

It never was supposed to be easy.
That's why all he asks of us is to be faithful.[40]
(And we won't even be that unless God helps us!)

C. Perfection
Psalms 119:96 (KJV)
I have seen an end of all perfection: but thy commandment is exceeding broad.

For ye are bought with a price: therefore glorify God in your body, and in your spirit, which are God's.
[37] 1 Peter 5:8 (KJV)
Be sober, be vigilant; because your adversary the devil, as a roaring lion, walketh about, seeking whom he may devour:
[38] 2 Timothy 2:3 (KJV)
Thou therefore endure hardness, as a good soldier of Jesus Christ.
[39] Matthew 6:13 (KJV)
And lead us not into temptation, but deliver us from evil: For thine is the kingdom, and the power, and the glory, for ever. Amen.
[40] 1 Corinthians 4:2 (KJV)
Moreover it is required in stewards, that a man be found faithful.

I understand that the Hebrew rendering of this first phrase would be something like, "**I have seen an end of the end**."

Perfection means eternity.
One of my favorite expressions for eternity is "**the consummation of all things.**" That's a pretty close interpretation of "*an end of all perfection*."

And then it finishes with, "*but thy commandment is exceeding broad.*"

Think of it like this
- **It is God's Word by which we are saved**
- **It is God's Word by which we are kept in this life and**
- **It is God's Word by which we will see God's plan come to fulfillment**

Chapter Fifteen
A SPIRITUAL RESET
Psalms 119:97-104 (KJV)

O how love I thy law! it is my meditation all the day.

Thou through thy commandments hast made me wiser than mine enemies: for they are ever with me.

I have more understanding than all my teachers: for thy testimonies are my meditation.

I understand more than the ancients, because I keep thy precepts.

I have refrained my feet from every evil way, that I might keep thy word.

I have not departed from thy judgments: for thou hast taught me.

How sweet are thy words unto my taste! yea, sweeter than honey to my mouth!

Through thy precepts I get understanding: therefore I hate every false way.

When we lived in Astoria, I would go fishing in the mouth of the Columbia with a guy named Ed Jasper. Brother Ed was probably 30 years older than me. I am pretty sure that the only reason he let me go fishing with him and his friends is that I was still young enough to pull the anchor whenever we needed to reposition the boat. Certain spots in the river were good holes to fish for the sturgeon. Brother Ed knew where those holes were and when we got to them, he'd set the anchor so we could fish down into them. But the constant current of the river, together with the rise and fall of the tide, would eventually cause the boat to shift, and we'd be in the same general vicinity of the fishing hole but no longer fishing in it. I don't recall exactly how often, but Brother Jasper would have me pull the anchor every so often. Then, he would reposition the boat and drop anchor again.

Every once in a while, a person needs to reset things on what matters spiritually.

It is very easy to:
- **keep doing all the things we usually do as Christians,**
- **keep doing them in the same general place we typically do them**
- **keep with the believers we would generally do them with**

But drift just enough off that we are no longer where we ought to be as believers.

We need to reposition ourselves and reset our anchor in Christ

That might be a good way to view this thirteenth stanza in the 119th Psalm.

See how the Psalmist begins, Psalms 119:97 (KJV)
O how love I thy law! it is my meditation all the day.

That is how to reset your life spiritually.

One writer said of this stanza, *"This is a pure song of praise. It contains no single petition, but is just one glad outpouring of the heart."* (Morgan)"[41]

CONTRASTS
Psalms 119:98-100 (KJV)
Thou through thy commandments hast made me wiser than mine enemies: for they are ever with me.
I have more understanding than all my teachers: for thy testimonies are my meditation.
I understand more than the ancients, because I keep thy precepts.

The Psalmist contrasts himself with three characters
A. His Enemies
Psalms 119:98 (KJV)

---

[41] https://www.blueletterbible.org/comm/guzik_david/studyguide2017-psa/psa-119.cfm

Thou through thy commandments hast made me wiser than mine enemies: for they are ever with me.

Notice the word "wiser."
It's not that there is no wisdom in this world.
But the wisdom of this world is foolishness to God.

The Word of God had given him better wisdom than his enemies had.

B. His Teachers
Psalms 119:99 (KJV)
I have more understanding than all my teachers: for thy testimonies are my meditation.

All of us have, even require, "influencers" in our lives who are supportive of us but may not be believers.[42]

- **Maybe a mentor who taught us our craft.**
- **Or a teacher at college**

They aren't enemies – they don't oppose our faith but are not spiritually on the same page.

We're going to have those relationships. A Spiritual reset would mean putting those teachers in their proper place in our lives. They should never be allowed to lead us a direction different than what the Bible teaches.

C. The Ancients
Psalms 119:100 (KJV)
I understand more than the ancients, because I keep thy precepts.

It's not limited to, but I can think of some people we might consider some great ancients:

---

[42] Or of the same Christian faith as we are.

- **Benjamin Franklin**
- **George Washington**
- **Thomas Jefferson**

These and the other founding fathers of our country were great men. We have much to be thankful for in them.

But I would rather stand in the ranks of an impoverished Baptist preacher any day of the week.
Because he has more of a spiritual understanding than any of those ancients.

CONSIDERATIONS
This stanza begins Psalms 119:97 (KJV)
O how love I thy law! ...

I wonder, what is your relationship with the Word of God?
There are at least four things our Psalmist says in consideration of the Word of God.
A. Love the Word
Psalms 119:97 (KJV)
O how love I thy law! it is my meditation all the day.

B. Meditate on the Word
Psalms 119:97 (KJV)
... it is my meditation all the day.

Psalms 119:99 (KJV)
... for thy testimonies are my meditation.

Meditation – serious thought.
The idea is to be "swept away" in thought.

He's focused!

C. Keep the Word
Psalms 119:100 (KJV)

I understand more than the ancients, because I keep thy precepts.

A **watchman**, a **guard**, or a **preserver**.
We need some believers today who will not only obey the Word of God but will also be zealous about getting others to obey the Word.

Don't get upset at your pastor because he's trying to hold you to a higher standard.

He just sees that people are claiming to love the Lord and believe the Bible, but whose spiritual life is slipping more and more quickly away from what the Bible teaches us.

D. Taste the Word
Psalms 119:103 (KJV)
How sweet are thy words unto my taste! yea, sweeter than honey to my mouth!

Far from being grievous, the commandments of the Word of God bring delight to the one who truly loved the Lord.[43]

CONSEQUENCES
There are three things this stanza says love for the Word of God will do:
A. Hate the false way
Psalms 119:104 (KJV)
Through thy precepts I get understanding: therefore I hate every false way.

Having something we love necessitates having another we hate.

---

[43] 1 John 5:3 (KJV)
For this is the love of God, that we keep his commandments: and his commandments are not grievous.

If we love the truth, we will hate what is false.

It doesn't mean hating people.
It means hating the wrong step and where it leads people.

B. Refrain from the evil way
Psalms 119:101 (KJV)
I have refrained my feet from every evil way, that I might keep thy word.

Having hated every false way, he has chosen not to walk in an evil way.

Notice he says, "every evil way."

Every one of them – regardless of what grade of evil.

The result was
C. He was not led astray
Psalms 119:102 (KJV)
I have not departed from thy judgments: for thou hast taught me.

This is the key.

1 Corinthians 10:12 (KJV)
Wherefore let him that thinketh he standeth take heed lest he fall.

It is the proud person who believes he can't fall.
Spiritually humble people take appropriate Bible steps to avoid departing from God's way.

That's a spiritual reset.

Chapter Sixteen

THE END

Psalms 119:105-112 (KJV)

Thy word is a lamp unto my feet, and a light unto my path.
I have sworn, and I will perform it, that I will keep thy righteous judgments.
I am afflicted very much: quicken me, O LORD, according unto thy word.
Accept, I beseech thee, the freewill offerings of my mouth, O LORD, and teach me thy judgments.
My soul is continually in my hand: yet do I not forget thy law.
The wicked have laid a snare for me: yet I erred not from thy precepts.
Thy testimonies have I taken as an heritage for ever: for they are the rejoicing of my heart.
I have inclined mine heart to perform thy statutes alway, even unto the end.

I want to take my cue for this lesson from verse 112 and the last phrase, "*...even unto the end.*"

I cannot tell you that this is the main theme of this stanza of the Psalm, but it is certainly a major one.[44]

This is the 14th stanza
There are 22 of them

Each stanza is 8 verses long
Each stanza correlates to one of the 22 letters in the Hebrew alphabet

---

[44] I do not know that there is a main theme. I would be tempted to use verse 105, "Thy word is a lamp unto my feet, and a light unto my path." But I am afraid I would do that because it is the verse most familiar, not because it is the "defining verse" of the passage.

If we were reading this in Hebrew we would discover that the first verse of each of these eight verses begins with the letter "nun" like our n.

I would like to deal with this passage under the heading, **What to do when you are at the end**

THE PSALMIST'S AFFLICTION
I found, I think eight times Psalms 119 uses the terms, afflict, afflicted or affliction.

The Psalmist was hurting.

He said of his affliction
A. It is very great
Psalms 119:107 (KJV)
I am afflicted very much: quicken me, O LORD, according unto thy word.

If this was you or me, I might wonder if he was exaggerating his problems?

We tend to do that, don't we?

Did you ever hear of the hypochondriac?
He complained so much about being sick that, after a while, nobody paid any attention to them anymore.

Years went on – each one with more and new complaints about how bad his health was.

After 7 or 8 decades of his complaining, he finally died.

For all of those years, eing sure he was going to die at any minute, he had made his own arrangements for his burial.

He ordered a grave marker with the words, "**I told you so.**"

The Psalmist wasn't exaggerating.
He was inspired by the Holy Spirit to express what he believed to be the absolute truth.

"I am afflicted very much."

B. It is the result of the wicked
Psalms 119:110 (KJV)
The wicked have laid a snare for me: yet I erred not from thy precepts.

- **His affliction was not the result of bad choices on his part.**
- **His affliction was not caused by poor living conditions.**

His affliction was specifically caused by the wicked.

You and I probably define that term more strictly than the Bible does.

The word wicked simply means "**one who has departed from the correct path.**"

That means a wicked person could be
- **As simple as a child who no longer obeys his parents.**
- **Or it could be someone who is a serial murderer.**

It is probably to our hurt that we tend to "grade" sin.
Some sins are considered almost "cute."

The Bible does not grade sin like that.
The homosexual was to be executed, so was the adulterer, and so was the rebellious child.

C. It is a deadly threat
Psalms 119:109 (KJV)

My soul is continually in my hand: yet do I not forget thy law.

Psalms 119:112 (KJV)
I have inclined mine heart to perform thy statutes alway, even unto the end.

He really did believe this could be the end of his life.

King David did experience some attacks that could have cost his life.

- **Saul**, whom David had once served, departed from God and attacked David.
- **Absalom**, David's own son, attempted to take the kingdom away from his father in a failed overthrow
- **Ahithophel**, who had been David's trusted counselor but turned against him to try to help Absalom.

THE PSALMIST'S INTENTION
There are three things he committed himself to:
A. I will keep thy judgments
Psalms 119:106 (KJV)
I have sworn, and I will perform it, that I will keep thy righteous judgments.

Notice the phrase, "I have sworn."
It's an oath.

It's better not to make an oath than to make one and not keep it.[45]

B. I will make my offerings
Psalms 119:108 (KJV)

---

[45] Ecclesiastes 5:5 (KJV)
Better is it that thou shouldest not vow, than that thou shouldest vow and not pay.

Accept, I beseech thee, the freewill offerings of my mouth, O LORD, and teach me thy judgments.

Freewill offerings, as far as we see them in the Bible.
Were always voluntary – the result of thanksgiving to God and
Were always given to the house of God – Tabernacle or Temple.[46]

C. I will perform thy statutes
Psalms 119:112 (KJV)
I have inclined mine heart to perform thy statutes alway, even unto the end.

The word perform, according to the Hebrew dictionary, is a generic word that always implies **action**.

The thing about commitments – we need to make them before the problem hits us. Otherwise, we will respond in a way that is mostly fleshly, not spiritual.

THE PSALMIST'S PROTECTION
He sees the Bible as His shield, his protection against the dangers he faced.

He says of the Word of God that it is
A. A lamp
Psalms 119:105 (KJV)
Thy word is a lamp unto my feet, and a light unto my path.

---

[46] 2 Corinthians 8:1-2 (KJV)
Moreover, brethren, we do you to wit of the grace of God bestowed on the churches of Macedonia;
How that in a great trial of affliction the abundance of their joy and their deep poverty abounded unto the riches of their liberality.

In those days a lamp would have been an oil filled container, with a wick.

A lamp is not the light. But it does make the light possible.

The Bible is not Jesus.
But without the Bible, we would not
- **Know Jesus**
- **See Jesus or**
- **Hear Jesus**

So that the Bible is also
B. A light
Psalms 119:105 (KJV)
Thy word is a lamp unto my feet, and a light unto my path.

John 1:1 (KJV)
In the beginning was the Word, and the Word was with God, and the Word was God.

The Word of God both shows us the Lord and is the Lord.

That's one of the reasons I do not believe it could have been possible for fallen man to corrupt the Word of God.

Satan has antichrists and false Christs, but he has not corrupted the Christ.

Finally, he says the Word of God is
C. A Heritage
Psalms 119:111 (KJV)
Thy testimonies have I taken as an heritage for ever: for they are the rejoicing of my heart.

This takes on a new meaning when you realize that he thought he was about to die.

A dying man said here, "I have something in the Word of God that will last me beyond the grave."

Therefore his heart rejoiced in the midst of affliction.

Chapter Seventeen
THE BASIS FOR A GODLY SPIRIT

Psalms 119:113-120 (KJV)
I hate vain thoughts: but thy law do I love.
Thou art my hiding place and my shield: I hope in thy word.
Depart from me, ye evildoers: for I will keep the commandments of my God.
Uphold me according unto thy word, that I may live: and let me not be ashamed of my hope.
Hold thou me up, and I shall be safe: and I will have respect unto thy statutes continually.
Thou hast trodden down all them that err from thy statutes: for their deceit is falsehood.
Thou puttest away all the wicked of the earth like dross: therefore I love thy testimonies.
My flesh trembleth for fear of thee; and I am afraid of thy judgments.

Someone once said, "Life is 10% what happens to you and 90% how you react to it."[47]

While I doubt that we would be able to quantify those percentages, the point is accurate enough.

Life happens whether we like it or not.

We did not choose for ourselves.
- **Our parents**
- **Our nationality**
- **Our standing**

We didn't even choose for ourselves to live.

We are thrust into life at the whim of a man and woman, and, we believe, the will of God.

---

[47] Attitude is everything quote from Charles Swindoll.

What happens from the moment of birth until the moment of death is a series of actions and reactions based upon our attitude.

The fifteenth of the twenty-two stanza's of Psalms 119 is a lesson in attitudes.

Notice how the Psalmist begins.
Psalms 119:113 (KJV)
I hate vain thoughts: but thy law do I love.

Hate and love – these are contrasting attitudes.

Diving into the stanza, we'll discover two other "complimentary" attitudes to go along with them.

I HATE
Psalms 119:113 (KJV)
I hate vain thoughts: ...

By the way, notice that, in this case, his hate came before his love.

It is not wrong to hate.
We just need to know what to hate – and the only proper judge of that is God, through His Word.

Have you ever seen the 6 or 9 graphic?
- **One person sees the 6**
- **The other person sees the 9**

There is only one way to determine which is correct – you must consult the originator.

I'm going to tell you – every problem we have in the world today is caused by people who refuse to consult the originator.

Even when it comes to understanding the Bible, the disagreements are the result of people debating what they see in the Bible rather than just letting God say what HE says in the Bible.

The Psalmist said he hates vain thoughts
Vain means empty – in this case, like double-minded.

I believe one of the keys to rightly dividing the Word of God is to see action or attitudes that appear to be directed at individuals in the Old Testament directed instead to our flesh in the New Testament.

We are to mortify the deeds of the body.[48]

With that in mind consider:
Psalms 119:115 (KJV)
Depart from me, ye evildoers: for I will keep the commandments of my God.
Remove[49] from our lives those things that are displeasing to the Lord.

Psalms 119:118 (KJV)
Thou hast trodden down[50] all them that err from thy statutes: for their deceit is falsehood.
Remove from our lives sins of ignorance and deceit.

Psalms 119:119 (KJV)
Thou puttest away all the wicked of the earth like dross: therefore I love thy testimonies.
Remove[51] from our lives hostility to God.

---

[48] Romans 8:13 (KJV)
For if ye live after the flesh, ye shall die: but if ye through the Spirit do mortify the deeds of the body, ye shall live.
[49] Dispose of
[50] Count and light and worthless
[51] Exterminate

I LOVE
Psalms 119:113 (KJV)
... but thy law do I love.

Psalms 119:117 (KJV)
Hold thou me up, and I shall be safe: and I will have respect[52] unto thy statutes continually.

The Psalmist says that he never takes his eyes off God's Word.
I don't believe that means he reads it without stopping, but that he studies it without stopping and never stops checking himself to see that he is observing them.

Psalms 119:119 (KJV)
Thou puttest away all the wicked of the earth like dross: therefore I love thy testimonies.

The Hebrew word for love means something akin to "a gift from God." We have this affection for the Word of God because we view it as given to us by God.

I HOPE
Psalms 119:114 (KJV)
Thou art my hiding place and my shield: I hope in thy word.

Psalms 119:116 (KJV)
Uphold me according unto thy word, that I may live: and let me not be ashamed of my hope.

The word hope means an expectation. It is to wait confidently, expecting the promise of God to come without delay.

---

[52] To gaze at

I AM AFRAID
Psalms 119:120 (KJV)
My flesh trembleth for fear of thee; and I am afraid of thy judgments.

The trouble in our world today is too little fear of the Lord.

Without that fear:
- **We have little knowledge**[53]
- **We have little wisdom**[54] **and**
- **We have a bad spirit**[55]

---

[53] Proverbs 1:7 (KJV)
The fear of the LORD is the beginning of knowledge: but fools despise wisdom and instruction.
[54] Proverbs 9:10 (KJV)
The fear of the LORD is the beginning of wisdom: and the knowledge of the holy is understanding.
[55] We don't hate, love, or hope for the right things

Chapter Eighteen
A TIME FOR ACTION
Psalms 119:121-128 (KJV)
I have done judgment and justice: leave me not to mine oppressors.
Be surety for thy servant for good: let not the proud oppress me.
Mine eyes fail for thy salvation, and for the word of thy righteousness.
Deal with thy servant according unto thy mercy, and teach me thy statutes.
I am thy servant; give me understanding, that I may know thy testimonies.
It is time for thee, LORD, to work: for they have made void thy law.
Therefore I love thy commandments above gold; yea, above fine gold.
Therefore I esteem all thy precepts concerning all things to be right; and I hate every false way.

We're looking at the sixteenth of the twenty-two stanzas' in Psalms 119 this morning.

I think I want to begin by pointing out what I thought about using as my title, a 3-2-2 equation in these verses
- **Three times we see the word, servant**
- **Two times we see the word, oppress and**
- **Two times we see the word, therefore**

Because he is a servant of the Lord and
Because he is facing oppression
Therefore, he asks God to act.

WHEN GOD'S WORD IS AVOIDED
Please look with me at, Psalms 119:126 (KJV)
It is time for thee, LORD, to work: for they have made void thy law.

This could be the rallying cry of every sincere believer today.
It is time for thee, Lord, to work.
Why?

For they have made void thy law.

It is worth considering, I think, who the "they" are.

It would make little sense that they would be the pagans, heathen, and Gentiles of David's day. They had never respected the Word of God ever.

His problem, just as it is in our time, is when those who profess to know the Lord, when those who ought to have known better, treat the Bible as if it has no use or say in their lives.

Think of how the Word of God was "avoided" in David's day:

- **When they chose a king instead of God as their head.**
- **When Saul chose to disobey God's Word and do what was Samuel's role to do**
- **When an entire army stayed true to Saul, in hunting down the man GOD had called to replace Saul**
- **When Joab murdered Abner against David's will**
- **When Amnon defiled his sister Tamar**
- **When Absalom led a rebellion against David**
- **When Adonijah assumed the right to be king even though God had called Solomon to the throne**

Sincere people, even believing people can fall into the same trap of making void the Word of God by avoiding the instructions or instructors of the Word of God.

- **When people hear the Word of God preached, but leave to continue doing what the Word teaches against**
- **When Christian knows what their pastor preaches, but choose to do contrary to his preaching**

One of the most grievous things we see right now is when preachers abandon what they were taught and promised to teach, to take

- **new doctrines,**
- **new practices and**
- **new fellowships**

It can be necessary to do those things, but they should be agonizing steps to take, and slow to be made.

When Christians reject the Word of God for their own opinions, ideas and lusts, it is time for God to work.

WHEN GOD'S SERVANTS ARE OPPRESSED
Psalms 119:121-122 (KJV)
I have done judgment and justice: leave me not to mine oppressors.
Be surety for thy servant for good: let not the proud oppress me.

Verse 122 is the only verse out of 176 in this Psalm, where the Word of God is not mentioned.

The mention in verse 121 is muffled to say the least.
If it is there it is in the phrase, *"I have done judgment and justice."*

God's Word is sometimes referred to as His judgments.

- No *judgment* **is right unless it is based upon the teaching of God's Word and**
- No *justice* **is possible unless it is aligned with the principles of God's word**

The Psalmist's only desire was to serve the Lord genuinely and fairly, according to what he understood to be the teaching of the Word of God, but proud people – those who did not believe they needed to obey the Word of God – oppressed him for it.

It was time for God to work
- **He was not going to take them on himself.**
- **He refused to lay his hands on King Saul**
- **He would not kill Abner, the general who took over Saul's army once he was dead**
- **He ordered that Absalom not be harmed even after he led an army against King David**

He would not counter-oppress his oppressors.
He left them, instead in the hands of God

WHEN GOD'S PEOPLE LOVE HIS PRECEPTS

Psalms 119:126-128 (KJV)
It is time for thee, LORD, to work: for they have made void thy law.
Therefore I love thy commandments above gold; yea, above fine gold.
Therefore I esteem all thy precepts concerning all things to be right;
and I hate every false way.

Mark well the contrast here
They have made void thy law
Therefore I love thy commandments above gold

They have made void thy law
Therefore I esteem all thy precepts concerning all things to be right

The more we see the Word of God ignored in our world today – The more we need to love it, obey it, preach it, teach it.

- **The more some professing Christians slip away from this or that lesson in the Bible**
- **The more we need to emphasize, not just the Word of God but ALL OF THE WORD OF GOD**

Chapter Nineteen
WONDERFUL

Psalms 119:129-136 (KJV)
Thy testimonies are wonderful: therefore doth my soul keep them.
The entrance of thy words giveth light; it giveth understanding unto the simple.
I opened my mouth, and panted: for I longed for thy commandments.
Look thou upon me, and be merciful unto me, as thou usest to do unto those that love thy name.
Order my steps in thy word: and let not any iniquity have dominion over me.
Deliver me from the oppression of man: so will I keep thy precepts.
Make thy face to shine upon thy servant; and teach me thy statutes.
Rivers of waters run down mine eyes, because they keep not thy law.

How many hours per week do you suppose you spend thinking about the things of this earth?[56]

There's really no way to escape it.

- **You had to think about earthly things just to drive to church today.**
- **If you work forty hours in a week, you had to mind the things of earth at least that long.**
- **Most of us have a house and a car and the payments that are generally associated with them. Those are the things of this earth.**

I'm thinking that, if we were to put it to pen and paper, we would be hard pressed to have our mind on heavenly things even a modest ten percent of the time.

What that suggests to me is that, those times we do mind heavenly things, what ought to give ourselves as fully as possible to it.

---

[56] Philippians 3:19 (KJV)
Whose end is destruction, whose God is their belly, and whose glory is in their shame, who mind earthly things.)

SOMETHING TO WONDER OVER
Psalms 119:129-130 (KJV)
Thy testimonies are wonderful: therefore doth my soul keep them.
The entrance of thy words giveth light; it giveth understanding unto the simple.

The ancient Hebrew pictograph was something like an open mouth

You know?
To be in awe at something.

It's jaw dropping.

Attached to the open mouth though, it a shepherd's staff.

A. Right away I think of being in awe with the Lord Jesus Christ.
Acts 1:10-11 (KJV)
And while they looked stedfastly toward heaven as he went up, behold, two men stood by them in white apparel;
Which also said, Ye men of Galilee, why stand ye gazing up into heaven? this same Jesus, which is taken up from you into heaven, shall so come in like manner as ye have seen him go into heaven.

I think sometimes we might think the angels rebuked them for gazing up into heaven. I don't think so.

Paul encouraged Christians
Titus 2:13 (KJV)
Looking for that blessed hope, and the glorious appearing of the great God and our Saviour Jesus Christ;

Everything we do in this world, we ought to do with our eyes *"stedfastly toward heaven."*

B. The word, wonderful has more meaning than just *wonderful*

The shepherd's staff reminds us of Jesus, our chief shepherd.

But the concept of the shepherd is one of authority or judgment.

God's testimonies are authoritative.

- **We ought to keep our eyes in the Word of God because they promise us of Jesus return and**
- **We ought to study them carefully and constantly because in God's Word we find His instructions for life.**

Psalms 119:130 (KJV)
The entrance of thy words giveth light; it giveth understanding unto the simple.

When God's word gets into us, they give light and they give understanding.

It's a lot easier to work on something when it is well lit.

C. No one can spend all their time in the Bible.
Everyone must spend a significant amount of their time minding matters of life.

But if, while we are in the word of God, we devote ourselves to it, we're going to find the matters of lifer much easier to mind.

SOMETHING TO LONG FOR
Psalms 119:131-132 (KJV)
I opened my mouth, and panted: for I longed for thy commandments.

Look thou upon me, and be merciful unto me, as thou usest to do unto those that love thy name.

There's a connection here between verse 129 and 131
- **In the first, the mouth is open, gazing**
- **In this, the mouth is open gasping**

The Psalmist presents a desperation for the Word of God.

It's because he knows he needs the Lord to see him and be merciful to him.

One of the great troubles in our world today is that so few see their need for mercy.

- **The one who is judgmental**
- **The one who is critical**
- **The one who gossips**

He is the one who believes he is beyond mercy.

Notice this insightful phrase, *"as though usest to do unto those that love thy name."*

We have a tendency to look at those believers of years gone by and think the God was better to them than He is to you and me.

- **God was better to the preachers in the 1950's**
- **God was better to Charles Hadden Spurgeon**
- **God was better to George Whitefield and John Wesley**
- **God was better to Elijah and Elisha**
- **God was better to this Psalmist (David**

than He is in our day.

But David looked back at perhaps
- **Joshua**
- **Moses**

- **Abraham and**
- **Noah**

And thought maybe God was better to them then than He was for him.

Here's the thing – that's not the right way to view the passage or to view the Lord.

What he means is "**God be merciful to me as You have proven Yourself always to be.**"

SOMETHING TO WEEP ABOUT
Psalms 119:133-136 (KJV)
Order my steps in thy word: and let not any iniquity have dominion over me.
Deliver me from the oppression of man: so will I keep thy precepts.
Make thy face to shine upon thy servant; and teach me thy statutes.
Rivers of waters run down mine eyes, because they keep not thy law.

I just want to point out the one thing that ought to cause a believer to weep – that there are souls that are not saved.

- **It's not the economy**
- **It's not the politics**
- **It's not the rumors of wars**

That should be a reason for tears.

- **We ought to weep that souls are lost[57] and**
- **We ought to weep that we are less effective in reaching souls[58] and then**

---

[57] Psalms 119:136 (KJV)
Rivers of waters run down mine eyes, because they keep not thy law.
[58] 2 Chronicles 7:14 (KJV)
If my people, which are called by my name, shall humble themselves, and pray, and seek my face, and turn from their wicked ways; then will I hear from heaven, and will forgive their sin, and will heal their land.

- We can rejoice that God promises we can win some of them.[59]

---

[59] Psalms 126:6 (KJV)

He that goeth forth and weepeth, bearing precious seed, shall doubtless come again with rejoicing, bringing his sheaves with him.

Chapter Twenty
THE ANSWER TO ANGUISH
Psalms 119:137-144 (KJV)

Righteous art thou, O LORD, and upright are thy judgments.

Thy testimonies that thou hast commanded are righteous and very faithful.

My zeal hath consumed me, because mine enemies have forgotten thy words.

Thy word is very pure: therefore thy servant loveth it.

I am small and despised: yet do not I forget thy precepts.

Thy righteousness is an everlasting righteousness, and thy law is the truth.

Trouble and anguish have taken hold on me: yet thy commandments are my delights.

The righteousness of thy testimonies is everlasting: give me understanding, and I shall live.

We come this morning to the 18th of 22 stanza's in Psalms 119.

Each of the stanza's corresponds to one of the 22 letters of the Hebrew alphabet.
- **Eight verses in each stanza**
- **Each verse of the stanza begins with the corresponding Hebrew letter**

God does use creativity and artistry of style to aide us in our comprehension and retention of His Word.

More significantly, all but one of the 176 verses of the Psalm contain some reference to the Word of God.

The Word of God is written about the Word of God!

We will never underestimate the importance of the Bible to our lives.
- **That's true both spiritually – it's how we get saved and grow in our relationship with God**

- **It's also true physically – it's how we learn to live with our fellow man**

Notice three things the Psalmist says about himself
My zeal hath consumed me,
Vs 139

I am small and despised
Vs 141

Trouble and anguish have taken hold on me
Vs 143

This stanza is an answer to help us deal with anguish and anxiety.

Let me say on the outset that anxiety is real. We ought not to ignore it or to be critical of those who face it.

But it does seem to be more of a problem in our world today than it was even 20 years ago.

That does not surprise me because our world is a much more evil place than it was 20 years ago.[60]

Christians are not immune to such anxiety.
Since we are the targets of so much of the evil intent of Satan and of unbelievers, it stands to reason we may face more of it than others.

I'll not mention a name just now, but one of my mentors in the faith went through severe and debilitating panic attacks.

- **We ought not to accuse people for having anxiety**
- **We cannot excuse[61] anxiety**

---

[60] The Bible confirms that it will become worse as time passes.

- **We need to**[62] **defuse the anxiety**

At the very least this stanza will provide tools to help.

THE RIGHTEOUSNESS OF THE LORD
Psalms 119:137 (KJV)
Righteous art thou, O LORD, and upright are thy judgments.

A. What's going on in the world is all right
I don't like very much of the stuff I see.
That is no reason to be angry with the Lord. He is righteous.

- **Why evil people get into office**
- **Why lifestyles that are abominable to God (and therefore to us) are promoted**
- **We good people, like police are defunded and derided**

These things all tend to create anxiety in us.
We know the Bible teaches against them. We know that God CAN prevent them.

Why doesn't He stop it?

It's critical that we settle in our soul that God is righteous in His dealings in this world.

B. What's going on with me
We all have
- **Prayers that are not answered the way we want them to be**
- **Choices we wish we did not have to make**[63]

---

[61] I mean by that, to ignore it and do nothing about it.
[62] By the grace of God
[63] I've been thinking lately that I wish I were either 45 or 74. If I were 44 I would not have to think about some of the things I do right now. If I were 74 I would have already gotten through some of the things I face right now. I don't have that option.

- **Circumstances we know God could wipe away for us if He would**

Trust God. Rest in Him.

He is righteous.
His judgments, His decisions, His dealings with the things that affect us are upright.

THE RIGHTEOUSNESS OF GOD'S WORD
Psalms 119:138 (KJV)
Thy testimonies that thou hast commanded are righteous and very faithful.

Psalms 119:140 (KJV)
Thy word is very pure: therefore thy servant loveth it.

It will seem counter-intuitive, but the more stressed and anxious a person becomes, they more they need to spend time in the Word of God.

It is a little like exercise.
It seems like it is wrong headed, but the more a body hurts, the more the body needs the exercise.

The less a person feels like exercising, the more the person needs to exercise.

Spiritually, the more anxious a person is, the more they need to love the Word of God.

The less a person feels like being in the Word of God, the more they need to do it.

- **The Word of God is right**
- **The Word of God is faithful[64]**

- **The Word of God is pure**

When everything around you seems evil and wrong, to focus on the one thing that is right, constant and absolutely pure, can calm the soul.

And just like exercise, it may seem like it doesn't do much good from one session to the next, but the cumulation of a life lived loving the Word of God will reap the reward of faith – less anxiety.

THE RIGHTEOUSNESS OF ETERNAL PROMISES

Psalms 119:142 (KJV)
Thy righteousness is an everlasting righteousness, and thy law is the truth.

Psalms 119:144 (KJV)
The righteousness of thy testimonies is everlasting: give me understanding, and I shall live.

Notice the word, everlasting.

It means without end, eternal...

Modern Christianity has done much disservice to believers by focusing Christianity on the immediate benefits.

No doubt there are some immediate benefits:
- **It is a healthier way to live**
- **It is a more peaceful way to live**
- **It is an honest way to live**
- **It is a friendly way to live**

---

[64] It does not change with the changing of time, circumstances or opinions of men.

The Bible teaches us
- **How to have better families**
- **How to be better stewards of our money**
- **How to be better workers on the job**
- **How to be better citizens in our country**
- **How to get along with people better**

The Bible teaches all those things. But they are secondary. The most important promises in the Bible are all eternal.

Jesus did not die on the cross so you can be healthier.

No one died for their faith so they could be better stewards of money.

It's like life insurance.
Some smart salesman figured out that no one would ever buy a product called "death insurance."
They came up with a fancy name, "life insurance" and marketed the notion that it was irresponsible and unloving to die without leaving something for those who live after you.

Some fancy Christian salesman did the same thing with Christianity. He figured out that fewer people would become professing Christians if all the promises were for after you die.

To get more followers, he reworded the message to focus on the benefits we can have right now. He marketed it in such a way that it became obviously successful. And people flocked to it.

The problem is, if your faith is only about what you can get out of it today, it's not going to help you much through the troubles of today.

The answer for anxiety is to trust God

- **Trust His judgments in life**
- **Trust His Word to help you and**
- **Trust His promises for all eternity**

Chapter Twenty-one

HOW HE HANDLED HIS LIFE OF TROUBLE

Psalms 119:145-152 (KJV)

I cried with my whole heart; hear me, O LORD: I will keep thy statutes.
I cried unto thee; save me, and I shall keep thy testimonies.
I prevented the dawning of the morning, and cried: I hoped in thy word.
Mine eyes prevent the night watches, that I might meditate in thy word.
Hear my voice according unto thy lovingkindness: O LORD, quicken me according to thy judgment.
They draw nigh that follow after mischief: they are far from thy law.
Thou art near, O LORD; and all thy commandments are truth.
Concerning thy testimonies, I have known of old that thou hast founded them for ever.

If I am correct that King David was the writer of Psalms 119, then David provides an interesting study into surviving tough times.

King David is one of the greatest of all heroes in the Bible. He was powerful and successful in so many ways.

But his was a life of struggle.
- **God gave him the work of combat.**
- **God gave him the duty to prepare a place of peace for King Solomon**

As a man of combat, David was almost constantly surrounded by enemies. He calls them in this stanza, *"they...that follow after mischief."*

I CRIED
Psalms 119:145-147 (KJV)

I cried with my whole heart; hear me, O LORD: I will keep thy statutes.
I cried unto thee; save me, and I shall keep thy testimonies.
I prevented the dawning of the morning, and cried: I hoped in thy word.

The word "cry" does not always mean with emotional distress.

- **A town crier, was simply one who announced important events and news**
- **A soldier might "sound the battle cry" in the sense of gathering troops for a cause**
- **A preacher is sometimes described as crying out the message of the Word of God**

To cry is to "call out."
But it can also be a "call for help."

Because of verse 147, I am under the impression this is of the emotional sort.
"I prevented the dawning of the morning, and cried: ..."

Ever been up all night crying?

God gives His beloved sleep.
But sometimes the trouble just won't let you close your eyes.

It's not sin to stay awake crying over hard things.

But David did not stay there.

I HOPED

Psalms 119:147-148 (KJV)
I prevented the dawning of the morning, and cried: I hoped in thy word.
Mine eyes prevent the night watches, that I might meditate in thy word.

It is in the same verse 147 that the Psalmist moves from crying to hope.

Don't feel guilty crying over trouble.
Just don't let that consume you.

There are three things the Psalmist says he did.

A. I waited on thy Word
(Stayed up at night)
Notice these two similar phrases
I prevented the dawning of the morning ... in thy Word[65]

Mine eyes prevent the night watches ... in thy Word

The staying awake has to do with waiting. He's on watch. It's his duty for the moment to be awake. But there is relief coming.

The relief comes in two forms
B. I hoped in thy word
That is an expectation.

Like the soldier on post through the night, he KNOWS there will be another to relieve him soon.

Listen, when we have that sort of confidence in the Word of God, it will get us through the difficult times.

It might be hard right now
You might wish you could get out of this right now

But rest assured, God has your back and His Word will not fail to provide relief.

---

[65] I'll focus on the part I skipped in a minute.

Therefore, the Psalmist said
C. I meditated in thy Word
Since the Word of God was his relief, he kept his thoughts upon it.

The Word of God will help any Christian through anything.

But only if we believe it, know it, and meditate upon it.

I PRAYED
Psalms 119:149-152 (KJV)
Hear my voice according unto thy lovingkindness: O LORD, quicken me according to thy judgment.
They draw nigh that follow after mischief: they are far from thy law.
Thou art near, O LORD; and all thy commandments are truth.
Concerning thy testimonies, I have known of old that thou hast founded them for ever.

Ok. Well, he didn't really say the words.

What he did was to pray...
"Hear my voice... O LORD"

I wrote this Daily Visit with the Lord Friday.
Romans 12:12 (KJV)
Rejoicing in hope; patient in tribulation; continuing instant in prayer;

I see this as something of a pyramid:

Rejoicing in hope
Patient in tribulation
Continuing instant in prayer

The foundation of the structure is prayer.
Without it, nothing else in this structure is possible.

Patience in tribulation is fundamental to faith.
All who live godly in Christ Jesus shall suffer persecution, so tribulation is part and parcel with the faith, and patience is key to its endurance.

Rejoicing in hope is that which is visible.
A prayer life, though sometimes public, is only truly effective when it is mostly secret between the believer and the Lord. If one is patient in tribulation, others will likely not notice.

So that which becomes the most visible aspect of faith is rejoicing in hope. Those who witness the believers who have it will likely only see their hopefulness and joy. Little will be made of their tribulations, and their secret prayer life - the thing that sustains them - is, well, secret.

It wouldn't be too hard to be jealous of these Christians because they appear happy and hopeful. If only others knew. They are as burdened as anyone else. They spend countless hours asking God for the strength to keep on in their trials. But, because God is faithful to answer their prayers, all most everyone else sees is their joy and hopeful expectation

Chapter Twenty-two
A BIBLICAL COUNTDOWN
Psalms 119:153-160 (KJV)

Consider mine affliction, and deliver me: for I do not forget thy law.
Plead my cause, and deliver me: quicken me according to thy word.
Salvation is far from the wicked: for they seek not thy statutes.
Great are thy tender mercies, O LORD: quicken me according to thy judgments.
Many are my persecutors and mine enemies; yet do I not decline from thy testimonies.
I beheld the transgressors, and was grieved; because they kept not thy word.
Consider how I love thy precepts: quicken me, O LORD, according to thy lovingkindness.
Thy word is true from the beginning: and every one of thy righteous judgments endureth for ever.

We're beginning our descent in this series from Psalms 119.

The Psalm is made up of
- **twenty-two stanzas, each one**
- **eight verses long and each verse**
- **beginning with the corresponding letter to the Hebrew alphabet**

This is stanza number twenty. Just two more left.

I believe I am going to bring a shorter series of lessons from the book of Jude. It is the only book of the New Testament I have not attempted to teach or preach through.

Getting closer to the end as we are, I think the title of this lesson is fitting.

Just as we are counting down in the Psalm, I find a "countdown" in this stanza.

FOUR ALLUSIONS TO AFFLICTION

A. God sees and helps us through affliction
Psalms 119:153 (KJV)
<u>Consider mine affliction</u>, and deliver me: for I do not forget thy law.

It is a wonderful comfort to know that God considers our times of affliction.
We are not alone in those times, though sometimes it feels like it.

It is even better to know that God delivers us from our times of affliction.
1 Corinthians 10:13 (KJV)
There hath no temptation taken you but such as is common to man: but God is faithful, who will not suffer you to be tempted above that ye are able; but will with the temptation also make a way to escape, that ye may be able to bear it.

I want you to know that there is a key to receiving this comfort and help.
He did not forget God's law.

B. The source of our affliction
Psalms 119:155 (KJV)
<u>Salvation is far from the wicked</u>: for they seek not thy statutes.

So much of the affliction we experience is because we live in a world filled with people who do not even try to obey
- **God's Word**
- **God's Laws or even**
- **God's principles**

None of us do it perfectly. They do not do it at all.

C. The spread of our enemies
Psalms 119:157 (KJV)
<u>Many are my persecutors and mine enemies</u>; yet do I not decline from thy testimonies.

Seems like persecutors and enemies are growing in numbers.

- **Used to be Christians were considered the bedrock of society**
- **Now we are considered the threat to society**

That, I notice, did not turn the Psalmist from the Word of God.

D. The sight of the Psalmist
Psalms 119:158 (KJV)
I beheld the transgressors, and was grieved; because they kept not thy word.

He could not help but to see them.
I do not believe it is healthy to keep our eyes on the transgressors, but we would be foolish to suggest we never see them.

THREE APPEALS FOR REVIVAL
The phrase used is "quicken me".
It means, **to have or to sustain life**.

The Psalmist prays for this quickening according to or based up three Biblical pedestals.
A. God's Word
Psalms 119:154 (KJV)
Plead my cause, and deliver me: quicken me according to thy word.

I'd take this two ways:
- **The Word of God as a whole**
- **The promises contained in the Word of God**

The Bible and revival go hand in hand.

B. God's Judgments
Psalms 119:156 (KJV)

Great are thy tender mercies, O LORD: <u>quicken me according to thy judgments.</u>

The decisions and choices and good understanding of God. A judge is supposed to be
- **knowledgeable of the law**
- **wise to exercise the law of good**

C. God's Lovingkindness
Psalms 119:159 (KJV)
Consider how I love thy precepts: <u>quicken me, O LORD, according to thy lovingkindness.</u>

- **God is not only omniscient and wise**
- **God is loving and kind**

We may expect the Lord to quicken and revive us, to sustain us and lift us simply because He is loving and kind.

TWO ANSWERS FOR THE WICKED

A. They are not saved
Psalms 119:155 (KJV)
<u>Salvation is far from the wicked: for they seek not thy statutes.</u>

The Psalmist said in another place Psalms 36:1 (KJV)
The transgression of the wicked saith within my heart, that there is no fear of God before his eyes.

I can only see the outward side of a man. I cannot see their heart, so I cannot say for certain whether a person is saved or not.

But I can say that those who do not seek God's statutes have no fear of God.

This is no reason to condemn them. The Psalmist also shows us

B. They need to be saved

Psalms 119:158 (KJV)
I beheld the transgressors, <u>and was grieved</u>; because they kept not thy word.

I...was grieved

Psalms 126:6 (KJV)
He that goeth forth and weepeth, bearing precious seed, shall doubtless come again with rejoicing, bringing his sheaves with him.

The spiritual man will always be grieved and weep for the lost.

ONE ASSERTION TO SUPPORT THE BELIEVER

Psalms 119:160 (KJV)
Thy word is true <u>from the beginning</u>: and every one of thy righteous judgments <u>endureth for ever.</u>

This verse is amazing to me.
Look at the phrases
- **From the beginning**
- **Endureth for ever**

I am reminded of Revelation 22:13 (KJV)
I am Alpha and Omega, the beginning and the end, the first and the last.

There is that unbreakable connection between the Word of God and the Lord Jesus Christ.

I want to finish by saying that the Bible is as true today, and will be as true tomorrow, as it was from the very beginning.

Chapter Twenty-three

THE RESPONSES OF A RIGHTEOUS MAN

Psalms 119:161-168 (KJV)

Princes have persecuted me without a cause: but my heart standeth in awe of thy word.
I rejoice at thy word, as one that findeth great spoil.
I hate and abhor lying: but thy law do I love.
Seven times a day do I praise thee because of thy righteous judgments.
Great peace have they which love thy law: and nothing shall offend them.
LORD, I have hoped for thy salvation, and done thy commandments.
My soul hath kept thy testimonies; and I love them exceedingly.
I have kept thy precepts and thy testimonies: for all my ways are before thee.

I think one of my favorite verses in the Bible is Psalms 119:165 (KJV)
Great peace have they which love thy law: and nothing shall offend them.

I am relatively certain I had read it many times[66] before the verse actually registered in my soul.
I remember being in the auditorium in our church, listening to a cassette tape of Evangelist Tim Lee[67] that missionary Joe Merlo gave me.
Brother Lee got to this verse and read it. *Great peace have they which love thy law:* **and nothing shall offend them.**

He began to go through a list of possible offenses:

---

[66] In the earliest days of my ministry, I read the Psalms through once a month. It's pretty easy to do if you read five Psalms a day.
[67] This illustrates the value of preaching in our lives. It's not the only tool God has given us, but Bible preaching amplifies the benefit of Bible reading, studying, and Bible memory.

Someone speaks unkindly of you -- **_and nothing shall offend them._**

Someone cuts you off at an intersection -- **_and nothing shall offend them._**

The pastor preaches a message that convicts you -- **_and nothing shall offend them._**

Someone at church gets to teach the class you wanted -- **_and nothing shall offend them._**

The Bible offers the righteous a series of responses much better than being offended.

POSTIVE RESPONSES TO THE WORD OF GOD

A. Awe
Psalms 119:161 (KJV)
Princes have persecuted me without a cause: but my heart standeth in awe of thy word.

I think when we generally think of the word "awe" we think of it as something we admire, or truly admire.

We'd be in awe if we were invited into the presence of one of our heroes.

Actually, the word means to fear, to tremble in our knees.

If we truly feared the Word of God, we would likely not be moved[68] much by the those who persecute us, even if we knew they had no reason.

B. Rejoice

---

[68] Offended

Psalms 119:162 (KJV)
I rejoice at thy word, as one that findeth great spoil.

The to rejoice is to celebrate.

The Word of God is such a prize, such a great find, nothing else compares to it, and no trouble can dim it's beauty.

It's not a weapon you must guard with your life.[69]
It's a treasure you cannot let go.

C. Love
The Psalmist uses the word love three times in these eight verses to describe his relationship with the Word of God.
Psalms 119:163 (KJV)
I hate and abhor lying: but thy law do I love.

Psalms 119:165 (KJV)
Great peace have they which love thy law: and nothing shall offend them.

Psalms 119:167 (KJV)
My soul hath kept thy testimonies; and I love them exceedingly.

I believe the Ancient Hebrew Lexicon is helpful –
"[The pictograph is composed of two symbols. The first,] represents one who is looking at a great sight with his hands raised as when saying, "Behold." The [second] is a representation of the tent or house.
Combined these pictures mean "look toward the house" or "provide for the family". One does not choose the household which one is born into, including tribe, parents, children and wife (as marriages were often arranged by the father), **it is a gift from God.** These gifts are seen as a privilege and are to be cherished and protected."

---

[69] As the minutemen did their weapons at Lexington and Concord.

The Bible is a gift from God,
- **to be cherished and protected,**
- **to be read and gazed into**
- **to be referenced, pointed to and shared with others**

D. Praise
Psalms 119:164 (KJV)
Seven times a day do I praise thee because of thy righteous judgments.

The Hebrew word for praise is very similar to love.
- **But instead of looking toward with hands uplifted and cherishing**
- **This is looking toward with hands uplifted and in that direction**

To praise God is to look to Him and press yourself and those you love toward Him.

He says he's going to do it seven times a day. The number seven often means perfection or completion.

He's not going to quit moving toward God until he reaches Him.

E. Peace
Psalms 119:165 (KJV)
Great peace have they which love thy law: and nothing shall offend them.

Look at the contrast between peace versus offence.
- **Peace: safety, happiness, contentment**
- **Offence: ruin, fail, fall**

The difference between ruin and safety is to love the Law of God.

F. Hope
Psalms 119:166 (KJV)
LORD, I have hoped for thy salvation, and done thy commandments.

It means to wait with confidence.
And while he waits, he obeys and keeps God's commandments.

When life is so hard you don't know what else to do, just do what the Bible says.

NEGATIVE RESPONSES AS A RESULT OF THE WORD OF GOD

Psalms 119:163 (KJV)
I hate and abhor lying: but thy law do I love.

It's obvious from the text that they go together.

There is nothing that can offend the righteous soul who loves and obeys the Word of God.

But there is something he should hate and abhor; **Lying**

I warn you not to hate anybody, not even the liar.

In the context of the Word of God that he says three times he loves, I believe what he hates and abhors is something other than the truth of God's word.

- **He avoids**
- **He shuns**
- **He refuses to listen to**

Teaching, counsel, directions, encouragement, philosophies, ideologies that are opposed to the Word of God.

If we will love the Word of God, and refuse the philosophies of men, we will find we have GREAT PEACE and no reason to be offended by the troubles we face.

Chapter Twenty-four

THE FOUR PRAYERS OF A RIGHTEOUS MAN

Psalms 119:169-176 (KJV)

Let my cry come near before thee, O LORD: give me understanding according to thy word.

Let my supplication come before thee: deliver me according to thy word.

My lips shall utter praise, when thou hast taught me thy statutes.

My tongue shall speak of thy word: for all thy commandments are righteousness.

Let thine hand help me; for I have chosen thy precepts.

I have longed for thy salvation, O LORD; and thy law is my delight.

Let my soul live, and it shall praise thee; and let thy judgments help me.

I have gone astray like a lost sheep; seek thy servant; for I do not forget thy commandments.

We've come to the end of our lessons from Psalms 119.

I've come to the place in life where, as much as I **detest**, dead and dry fake Christianity, I **loathe** shallow faith.

I believe it is the reason for what the Bible clearly says will be the decline of faith in the end days.[70]

Just because Jesus said it would happen does not mean you and I must contribute to the problem.

- **Psalms 119 is smack dab in the middle of your Bible.**
- **It is the longest chapter in the Bible and**
- **Its subject IS the Bible[71]**

---

[70] Luke 18:8 (KJV)

I tell you that he will avenge them speedily. Nevertheless when the Son of man cometh, shall he find faith on the earth?

[71] One hundred seventy-six verses, all but one directly speaking of the Bible.

I am telling you; it is the Bible that we need.

- **We do not need programs, we need the Bible**
- **We do not need conferences, we need the Bible**
- **We do not need counseling models, we need the Bible**
- **We do not need diplomas and degrees, we need the Bible**

The Psalmist went to great lengths to make much of the Word of God.

- **One seventy-six verses**
- **Organized into twenty-two stanzas**
- **Each stanza exactly eight verses**
- **Each stanza corresponding to one of the twenty-two letter in the Hebrew alphabet**
- **Each verse in each stanza beginning with the corresponding Hebrew letter**

This was not thrown together on the fly. It was not sloppy work. It was thought out, prayed over, probably re-worked a few times.[72]

And yet, notice that the very last verse of this very careful piece of Scripture says, Psalms 119: 176 (KJV)
I have gone astray like a lost sheep; seek thy servant; for I do not forget thy commandments.

The greatest of all believers must admit that they have not attained in this life the thing God has for them to attain.

There are in these eight verses, four prayers

LET MY CRY
Psalms 119:169 (KJV)
Let my cry come near before thee, O LORD: give me understanding according to thy word.

---

[72] I speak as a man. I do recognize that the Holy Spirit of God could have inspired him so directly that this flowed out as if dictated by the Spirit of the Living God. But that highlights my point even more so.

When our boys were young we took them to a civil war reenactment at Fort Stevens outside of Astoria.

At the time, they were both that age where they thought being a soldier would be a really cool thing.[73]

We were sitting in the bleachers, just one step away from the battlefield action. A soldier was shot directly in front of us and re-enacted to the best of his ability what it might have been like to be struck by a 58 caliber minie-ball.

The man went to the ground not 10 feet in front of us and began to scream in agony and pain.

Bohannan was shocked, almost offended and asked us why he was behaving like that.

I told him that is probably more like what combat is than the clean, quick, romantic deaths kids pretend in their battle scenes.[74]

We are to "endure hardness as good soldiers of Jesus Christ.[75]

The battle that the Christian is called to fight
- **Is not romantic**
- **Is not clean and**
- **Is not quick**

We're just pretending if we can do it without sometimes crying out to God in pain.

---

[73] Every boy just about thinks about being a soldier, plays war.

[74] "Bang bang, you're dead. Now lay down."

[75] 2 Timothy 2:3 (KJV)
Thou therefore endure hardness, as a good soldier of Jesus Christ.

LET MY SUPPLICATION
Psalms 119:170-172 (KJV)
Let my supplication come before thee: deliver me according to thy word.
My lips shall utter praise, when thou hast taught me thy statutes.
My tongue shall speak of thy word: for all thy commandments are righteousness.

A supplication is a specific kind of prayer asking for God's favor or grace.

Asking God's favor in your life is not necessarily a selfish thing.

I'm thinking of Noah.

The Bible says, Genesis 6:8 (KJV)
But Noah found grace in the eyes of the LORD.
God showed him favor and
- **Spoke to him**
- **Gave him the supernatural ability to build the ark and to get the animals onto it**
- **His family was saved and**
- **He was saved**

But God did not give Noah grace just he could testify that he and his family had been blessed by God.

Noah was a preacher of righteousness.

God showed Noah favor so souls would have the opportunity to be saved.

The Psalmist says
- **My lips shall utter praise**
- **My tongue shall speak of thy Word**

That's the reason we seek the favor of the Lord.

LET THINE HAND
Psalms 119:173-174 (KJV)
Let thine hand help me; for I have chosen thy precepts.
I have longed for thy salvation, O LORD; and thy law is my delight.

The word help means to surround and to support.

The Bible says, *"vain is the help of man."*[76]

- **Wise businessmen**
- **Wise leaders**
- **Wise politicians**

surround themselves with good men.

A wise Christian knows better. He surrounds himself with the hand of God.

LET MY SOUL LIVE
Psalms 119:175-176 (KJV)
Let my soul live, and it shall praise thee; and let thy judgments help me.
I have gone astray like a lost sheep; seek thy servant; for I do not forget thy commandments.

We are in the last two verses of the Psalm, and I believe the point it to bring us to the most important truth the human soul can hear.

We have gone astray from God.[77]
We come short of the glory of God.[78]

---

[76] Psalms 60:11 (KJV)
Give us help from trouble: for vain is the help of man.
[77] Isaiah 53:6 (KJV)
All we like sheep have gone astray; we have turned every one to his own way; and the LORD hath laid on him the iniquity of us all.
[78] Romans 3:23 (KJV)

Each one of us is destined for eternal hell.[79]

God laid on Jesus the iniquity of us all so that, through the Word of God we might learn the way our soul may live forever.[80]

For all have sinned, and come short of the glory of God;
[79] Romans 6:23 (KJV)
For the wages of sin is death; but the gift of God is eternal life through Jesus Christ our Lord.
[80] [80] Isaiah 53:6 (KJV)
All we like sheep have gone astray; we have turned every one to his own way; and the LORD hath laid on him the iniquity of us all.

Thank you for reading my book.

I trust it has proven to be helpful and a blessing to you. Please forgive those typographical and grammatical mistakes you will no doubt come upon. While I have proofread for publication, I am sure I have missed many mistakes. In order to keep the price of the book low, I have elected not to pay for editing. I am always looking for those who would team with me to make editing suggestions. You will also see that I have developed my own style of writing for sermon preparation. It seems to work well for me as I preach from the pulpit. I have elected to keep most of that style intact. I trust it will add rather than distract from the effectiveness while you read.

Should you find the book is helpful to you, or if you have questions you would like to ask me, feel free to contact me.

My e-mail address is marvin@marvinmckenzie.org.
My books and other sources of content I have created may be found at marvinmckenzie.org.

You might also enjoy taking a look at the following:
www.bbcpuyallup.org
Daily Visit With God
http://mckenzie-visit-with-god.blogspot.com/

Buy me a coffee?

https://ko-fi.com/marvinmckenzie14276

The link to Ko-fi is an opportunity to support this effort to reach a world of souls with the Word of God. I would appreciate any gift you can give.

Made in the USA
Middletown, DE
02 June 2024

55138795R00080